How do things grow?

Dorling **DK** Kindersley

LONDON, NEW YORK, SYDNEY, DELHI, PARIS, MUNICH and JOHANNESBURG

Project Editors: Judith Hodge, Dawn Rowley,
Angela Wilkes, Sue Malyan
Project Art Editors: Catherine Goldsmith
Penny Lamprell, Rebecca Johns
Senior Editor: Sarah Levete
Editor: Anna Lofthouse
Senior Art Editor: Adrienne Hutchinson
Art Editor: Emy Manby
Managing Editors: Linda Martin, Mary Atkinson
Managing Art Editor: Peter Bailey
Senior DTP Designer: Bridget Roseberry
Production: Erica Rosen
Picture Researchers: Neale Chamberlain,
Angela Anderson, Marie Osborn
Computer-generated artwork: Alternative View
Photography: Steve Gorton, Gary Ombler
Jacket Designers: Karen Burgess, Sophia Tampakopoulos

First published in Great Britain in 2001 by
Dorling Kindersley Limited
80 Strand, London, WC2R ORL

2 4 6 8 10 9 7 5 3 1

A CIP catalogue record for this book is available from the British Library

ISBN 0-7513-1250-9

Colour reproduction by Colourscan, Singapore
Printed and bound in Italy by L.E.G.O.

The publisher would like to thank the following for
their kind permission to reproduce their
photographs:
a=above; c=centre; b=below; l=left; r=right; t=top

Bruce Coleman Ltd: Jules Cowan 19br; **Bruce**
Coleman Ltd: Hans Reinhard 26bl; Kim Taylor 29tl;
Geoff Ward: 31c; **Gettyone Stone:** 25tl; **N.H.P.A.:**
Suzanne Danegger 23br; David Woodfall 21tr;
Oxford Scientific Films: Breck Kent 33cl; **Planet
Earth Pictures:** Adam Jones 26cr; Andrey
Zvoznikov 17tr; Murray Cooper 29bl; Tom

Brakefield 33br; **Robert Harding Picture
Library:** 15tr; **Robert Harding Picture Library:**
19tl; **Telegraph Colour Library:** Arthur Tilley 3br;
Woodfall Wild Images: David Woodfall 32bl.

see our complete catalogue at **www.dk.com**

Experiments in Science

How do things grow?

written by David Glover

DK

A Dorling Kindersley Book

Contents

Living and Growing

Your Body

Plants

Exploring Nature

Hello!

I'm Chip!

I'm Pixel!

Meet Chip, Pixel and their helpful dog, Newton. Join these three friendly characters as they take you on an exciting and fact-filled journey of scientific discovery.

Grrrr, I'm Newton!

Before you begin

You'll need an adult to help you with the experiments in this book. Before starting, read the introduction, the list of equipment and the instructions. Make sure you look at the numbers on the instructions – they'll help you follow the steps one by one.

After reading the instructions, try to work out what you think will happen. After the experiment, think back to what you predicted. Did it happen as you expected?

Your scientific equipment

Look for the box like this by each experiment. Inside, you'll find a list of all the equipment you'll need – but remember to ask an adult before you use anything.

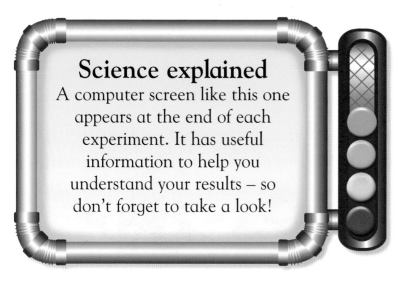

Science explained

A computer screen like this one appears at the end of each experiment. It has useful information to help you understand your results – so don't forget to take a look!

Science in real life

For each experiment, there's a photo showing a real-life example of the science that you're investigating. Can you think of any more real-life examples?

Extra information

At the back of the book, you'll find a glossary that tells you the meanings of new words. There's also an index to help you find your way around the book.

For your helper

Each section of this book has parents' notes especially for the adult who's helping you. The parents' notes for Living and Growing are on pages 16–17, Your Body are on pages 42–43, Plants are on pages 68–69 and Exploring Nature are on pages 94–95.

Get experimenting and have fun!

Test your knowledge

When you've finished all the experiments in each section, find out how much you remember by doing the fun quiz at the end.

Science safety

Science experiments are fun, but you still need to take care. Read through the instructions with an adult to see where you might need help.

Be especially careful when using any sharp tools, such as scissors. Always use round-ended scissors and, if necessary, ask an adult to help you.

Whenever you see this symbol, you should take extra care and always ask an adult for help.

Living and Growing

Parents' notes

This section will help your child to learn about the differences between living things and things that have never been alive. It will also develop your child's understanding of life processes. Read these notes and any on the relevant pages to help your child get the most out of the experiments.

Pages 18–19: Is it alive?

Discuss with your child why he or she has listed a particular item under living or non-living. Explain that although an item may fulfil some of the criteria on the checklist, this does not necessarily mean that it is living – for example, a bicycle moves but is not living.

Pages 20–21: Special parts

This activity will help your child to name and recognise the parts that make up a particular animal's body. Discuss what each body part is used for. Encourage him or her to experiment, adding different parts, such as a tail, to the animal. Help your child to name an animal that has those particular body parts.

Pages 22–23: Eating

This game of snap encourages your child to think about whether an animal is a meat-eater, a plant-eater or eats both meat and plants. If appropriate for your child, introduce the words *carnivore*, *herbivore* and *omnivore*. You may need to explain that in some food chains some animals become food for other meat-eating animals.

Pages 24–25: Growing

Make sure that there are several people of different ages from whom your child can take handprints. Encourage your child to look at different animals and to suggest how much they have grown or may grow.

Pages 26–27: Moving

The activities on these pages will encourage your child to observe the different ways in which animals move. When each model is complete, ask your child to name an animal with the same number of legs. Discuss together other special body parts used for movement, for example, wings and fins.

Pages 28–29: Sensing the world

Discuss with your child how he or she senses the surrounding world. Extend this discussion to include other animals, focusing on how and why they are sensitive to their surroundings. Make sure you supervise your child when he or she is near the open window. It is important your child understands why he or she should treat all animals with respect.

Pages 30–31: Animal disguise

The activity on these pages demonstrates to your child how an animal's appearance, such as its colour and skin pattern, can help it to blend in with its surroundings. Your child may need help in choosing an appropriate background. Encourage your child to suggest reasons why a particular animal needs to camouflage itself. You may need to explain further that camouflage can protect an animal from danger as well as enabling it to surprise its prey.

Pages 32–33: Animal homes

Accompany your child when he or she goes outside to check the flowerpot. Reassure him or her that any animals that have made a temporary home in the pot will soon find other homes. Explain why it is important to treat animals gently. Discuss why many animals find or build homes, for example to provide shelter and a safe place to rear young.

Pages 34–35: Laying eggs

Here your child can see that young brine shrimps hatch from eggs. Once the shrimps have hatched, you may like to put them into an aquarium or into a pond. Make sure that your child treats the brine shrimps with respect.

Pages 36–37: Life cycles

This activity focuses on the life cycles of a butterfly and a frog. Ask your child to suggest some reasons why the body of the growing animal changes and how it is then suited to its habitat. Encourage your child to think of the life cycles of other animals, including humans.

Is it alive?

Do you know which things are living and which things are not? Plants and animals are living. Animals move around, eat food and have babies. Plants grow leaves, use water, air and sunlight to make food, and make new plants from seeds.

Now make a chart
You will need: ★ a large piece of card
★ felt-tip pens ★ a ruler

Alive | Not alive

1 Make a chart like this one. Draw two columns, one for living things and one for things that are not alive.

2 Look at different things inside and outside your home. Can you find about 20 different things?

Jumping for life

People are alive. Like other animals, we move by ourselves, eat and grow. We can jump over a skipping rope, like this girl – but the skipping rope can't do any of these things – it is not living.

Science explained

Things made from stone, wood, cloth or plastic are not alive. These things do not eat, grow or have young. Plants are alive. They grow and make new plants. Any animals you listed on your chart, such as dogs and people, are alive. They move, grow, have young or reproduce.

3 Use this checklist to help you decide which things are alive and which things are not alive.

Checklist

Living things – animals
move
grow
drink and eat
have babies

Living things – plants
grow
need water and light
make new plants

Things that are not alive
do not eat
do not grow
do not have young

4 Write the names of things in the correct columns on your chart, like Chip is doing.

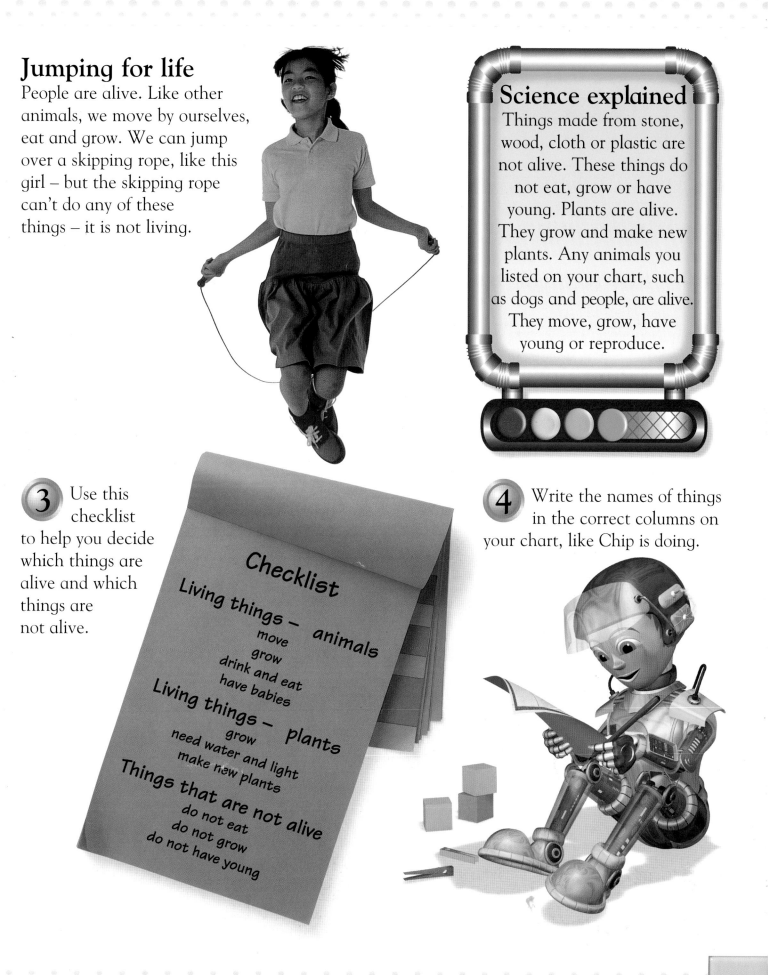

Special parts

Most animals have eyes to see, a mouth to eat with and ears to hear. Some animals have claws to dig and tails to swish away flies. Can you name an animal with a pouch or one with a trunk? What are these body parts used for?

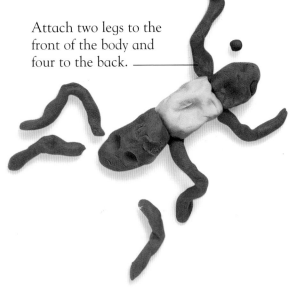

Now make an animal
You will need: ★ a large ball, or several small pieces, of modelling clay or pastry

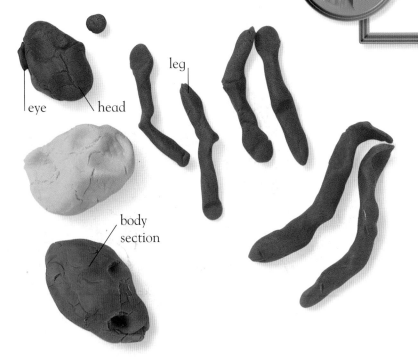

eye   head

leg

body section

Attach two legs to the front of the body and four to the back.

1 Mould the clay into two chunky sections for the animal's main body section. Make six leg shapes, a head and two small eye shapes.

2 Join up the two body sections. To complete the animal's body, add on the head, legs and eyes.

Under a shell

A crab has a hard shell to protect its body. Its eyes are on stalks so that it can safely take a peep at the outside world when it is hiding in a hole. It picks up food with special claws, called pincers.

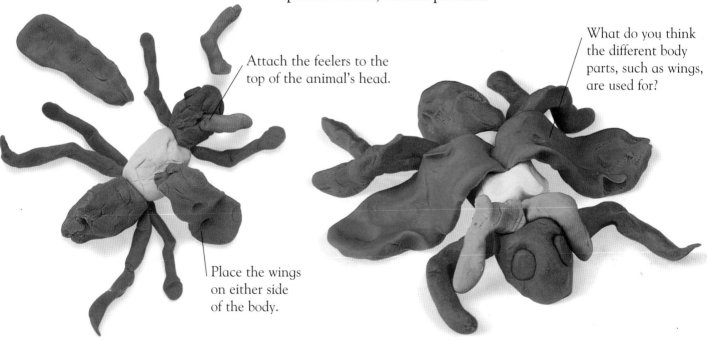

Attach the feelers to the top of the animal's head.

Place the wings on either side of the body.

What do you think the different body parts, such as wings, are used for?

3 Shape some more clay into two wings and two feelers. Attach the wings and feelers to the body, as shown.

4 Look at your finished animal. Now try to make an animal with four legs and no wings. What animal is it?

21

Eating

Animals must eat to live and grow. But different animals like different foods. Dogs love meat, but if you offer meat to a horse, it will turn its head away. Some animals eat only meat, others eat only plants, and some eat both.

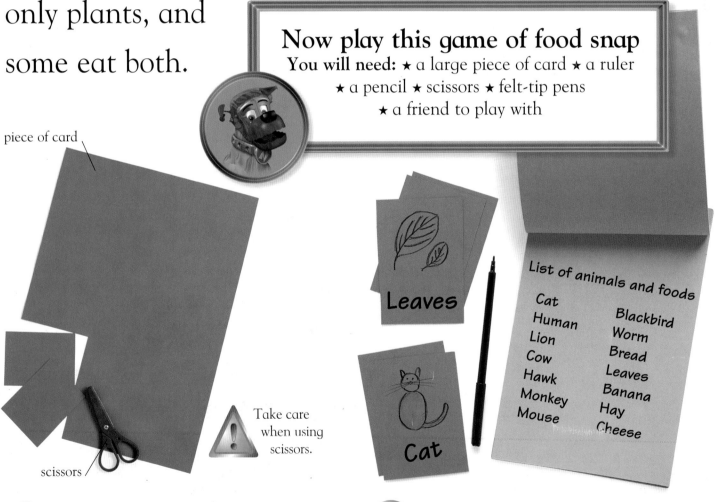

Now play this game of food snap
You will need: ★ a large piece of card ★ a ruler ★ a pencil ★ scissors ★ felt-tip pens ★ a friend to play with

piece of card

Leaves

Cat

scissors

Take care when using scissors.

List of animals and foods

Cat
Human
Lion
Cow
Hawk
Monkey
Mouse

Blackbird
Worm
Bread
Leaves
Banana
Hay
Cheese

1 Ask an adult to help you cut out 14 pieces of card, each about 8 cm (3 in) by 5 cm (2 in).

2 On each card, write the name of one of the animals or foods listed above, and draw a picture of it. Ask your friend to help.

Picky pandas

The giant panda is one of the rarest animals in the world. It lives in bamboo forests and likes to munch on tasty bamboo shoots and roots.

Science explained

Lions and cats are meat-eaters. Cows and worms are plant-eaters that never eat meat. Humans, mice and monkeys eat both plants and animals. A blackbird likes a juicy worm, but it must watch out for hawks, or it will be eaten itself!

3 Shuffle the cards, and deal them out equally between you and your friend. Keep the cards face down. Together with your friend, turn over one card each.

4 Call "snap" if the cards show an animal and a food that the animal eats. The person who calls "snap" correctly the most times is the winner.

Call "snap" when you see an animal card that matches a food card.

Snap!

Growing

It's hard to believe that a tiny acorn will grow into a huge oak tree or that a small puppy can grow into a big, strong dog. Living things grow bigger as they get older.

Now make some handprints to see how people grow.

Now make some handprints

You will need: ★ an apron ★ some newspaper ★ non-toxic liquid poster paint ★ a paintbrush ★ an old, plastic plate ★ several sheets of paper ★ a pencil ★ friends of different ages to help

newspaper   paper   paintbrush

plastic plate

liquid poster paint

1 Put on an apron and cover the table with newspaper. Now you are ready to start your handprinting.

2 Squeeze some poster paint onto the plate. Spread the paint evenly with the paintbrush.

paintbrush

Getting bigger

A baby elephant looks just like a small copy of its mother. In 25 years time, this baby will have grown as big as its mother.

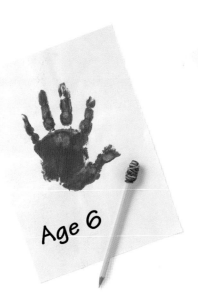

Age 6

Age 11

Age 7

Age 30

Age 4

3 Press your hand onto the paint, and then onto the paper to make a print. Wash the leftover paint from your hand. Label the handprint with your age.

4 Now ask other children, teenagers and adults to make their handprints. Label each print with the age of the person. Now look at the prints. What do you notice?

Moving

How many ways can you move? Can you crawl, walk, skip, hop and run? Can you swim in the sea or fly through the air? Animals move in different ways. Some slither over the ground, others have legs to walk, flippers to swim or wings to fly.

cardboard tube

bendy straw

card

sticky tape   scissors

Now make moving animals
You will need: ★ differently sized cardboard tubes ★ scissors ★ bendy straws ★ sticky tape ★ a piece of card

⚠ Take care when using scissors.

2 Cut out four feet shapes from the card, and tape one to each leg. Use the bends in the straws to make the animal walk. Move the legs forward, one after the other.

How easy is it to make your animal stand up or balance?

1 First make a four-legged animal. Use a long cardboard tube for the body and straws for the legs. Use the sticky tape to attach the legs to the body.

Wait for me!

Horse power
When a horse walks slowly, it lifts one leg at a time. When it gallops fast, it moves all four legs together.

3 Now try making an animal with two legs and another with six legs. Again, use card to make feet for your animals. Try making these animals walk. Which animal is the easiest to balance?

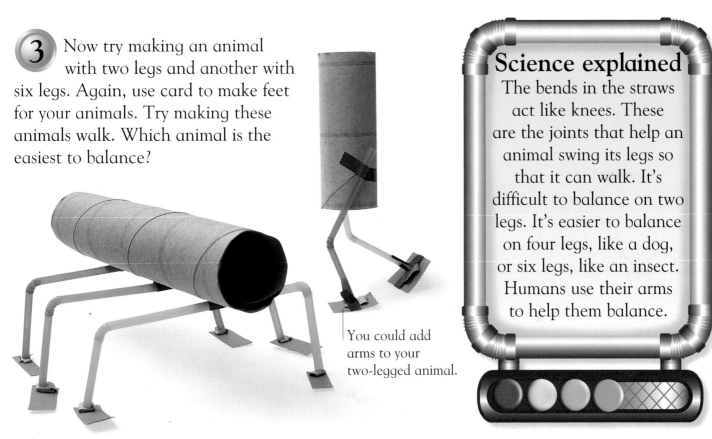

You could add arms to your two-legged animal.

Science explained
The bends in the straws act like knees. These are the joints that help an animal swing its legs so that it can walk. It's difficult to balance on two legs. It's easier to balance on four legs, like a dog, or six legs, like an insect. Humans use their arms to help them balance.

27

Sensing the world

Which do you like best – light or dark places, hot or cold places? Worms like to bury themselves in damp, dark soil, but some snakes like to bask in the hot sun. Animals can sense the world around them. They try to find a place where they can find food and feel safe and comfortable.

Now try this test

You will need: ★ scissors ★ a cardboard box ★ a bright torch ★ sticky tape ★ a dish ★ some slices of apple

cardboard box

torch

scissors

1 Cut a hole in one end of the box. Make sure it is just big enough for the torch to fit through.

Take care when using scissors.

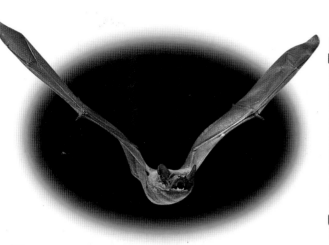

Science explained

Moths and other night insects use their eyes to find their way by the moonlight and starlight. The bright torch light confuses the insects. They fly in circles around it. They may smell the apple slices and stay in your box to have a feast!

Big ears

Bats fly at night, searching for food. They find their way by squeaking and listening for the echoes with their large ears.

2 On a warm evening, as it begins to get dark, put the box outside or near an open window. Ask an adult to help you. Put the dish of apples in the bottom of the box. Tape the torch in place so that it lights up the inside of the box.

Put the slices of apple in a dish.

3 Turn on the torch and turn off any other lights. With an adult, watch your box as it gets dark outside. Do any insects come to the light?

When you have finished watching, turn off the torch and let the insects fly away.

Animal disguise

Do you know why a zebra is stripy? The answer is that a zebra's stripes help to disguise, or camouflage, it in the wild. The stripes break up the zebra's outline, making it hard for a lion to spot it in the long grasses and bright sunshine.

Now disguise some animals
You will need: ★ a large piece of card ★ coloured pencils ★ scissors ★ double-sided sticky tape

coloured pencil

scissors

Take care when using scissors.

material

tree bark

pebble

1 Draw some animal shapes on the card. You could choose butterfly, lizard and fish shapes. Cut out the shapes.

2 Think about where you want your animals to be camouflaged. What about on a tree trunk, on some stones or even on some material?

What can you see?

It's hard to spot this slithery snake because its skin pattern blends in with the background. This camouflage makes it easy for the snake to sneak up on other animals, without it being seen first.

3 Colour the animal shapes in the colours of the places you have chosen to put the animals. Draw the colours in either stripy, patch or spot patterns.

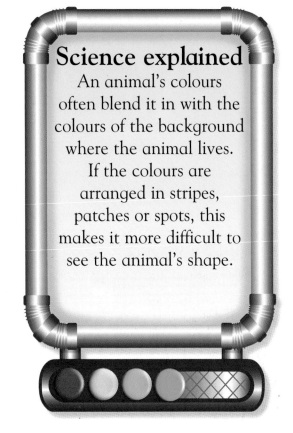

Science explained

An animal's colours often blend it in with the colours of the background where the animal lives. If the colours are arranged in stripes, patches or spots, this makes it more difficult to see the animal's shape.

4 Attach each animal to its background with sticky tape. Is it easy to spot your animal or is it too well camouflaged?

Animal homes

It's not just people who build homes. Birds build nests in which to lay their eggs and look after their young. Insects such as ants and bees live together in nests, like cities, ruled by a queen. Some fish make nests on the bottom of streams and keep guard until their young are born.

Now try this test
You will need: ★ a clay flowerpot
★ a small stone ★ a torch
★ a sheet of paper ★ a pencil

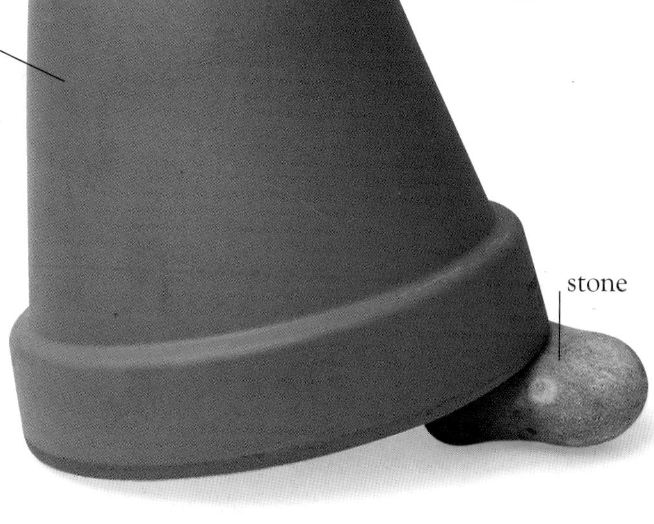

flowerpot

1 With an adult's help, find a shady corner near your home. This could be at the edge of a flowerbed or by the front door. Turn the flowerpot upside down and prop it up with the stone.

stone

A cosy home

This mouse has made itself a warm, dry nest of leaves. Here it can sleep comfortably, tucked up safely and out of the way of other animals.

Science explained

You may find a snail, woodlouse or a spider inside the pot. These small animals like to find dark, damp holes or spaces in which to hide. Snails will spend the night in the pot, and then crawl out during the day to feed on plants.

Shine the torch inside the flowerpot.

3 Check the pot in the daylight. Are the animals still there? Are there any new ones?

After you have finished, put the pot away. The animals will soon find a new home.

2 Leave the pot for a day or two. After dark, go outside with an adult and use a torch to see if any animals have made their home in the pot. Write down the name of each animal, the date and the time. Put the pot back.

Record your findings on your paper.

Laying eggs

Living things reproduce, which means that they have young that grow up to be like themselves. Some animals, such as humans, cats and dolphins, have babies that grow inside the mother's body. However, birds and many fish and reptiles lay eggs from which the babies hatch.

Now hatch some eggs
You will need: ★ a jug of 500 ml (18 fl oz) of warm water ★ a large jar ★ 50 g (2 oz) of sea salt ★ fish food ★ brine shrimp eggs bought from a pet shop ★ a magnifying glass ★ a teaspoon

warm water

1 Stir the salt into the warm water until all the salt has dissolved. Let the water cool to room temperature. Add a few pinches of fish food.

teaspoon

large jar

sea salt

fish food

2 Sprinkle a teaspoonful of eggs onto the water. Now leave the eggs to hatch. It will take about two days.

Cracking open

A duckling pushes its way out of an egg when it is ready to hatch. Ducklings can't look after themselves. They can swim almost as soon as they are born, but they stay with their mother until they have learned to find food and fly.

3 Over a sink, take out a teaspoonful of liquid and look carefully through the magnifying glass. What can you see?

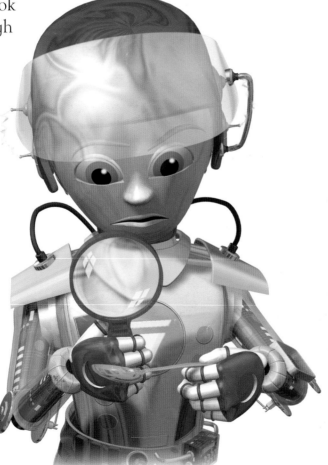

Science explained
The warm salt water is just right for the eggs to develop and hatch. The young that hatch are called larvae. They slowly change into adults. Feed the tiny animals with fish food. When you have finished studying the brine shrimps, put them into an aquarium or a pond.

Life cycles

A new life begins when an animal is born. It then grows up, learns to look after itself and has babies of its own. These stages that an animal goes through make up its life cycle. Animals grow old and die, but the young they leave behind carry on the cycle.

Now follow a butterfly's life cycle
You will need: ★ a piece of card
★ felt-tip pens ★ round-ended scissors

egg

caterpillar

chrysalis

butterfly

1 These photographs show the stages in the life cycle of a butterfly. Draw each stage on the card.

frogspawn

tadpole

frog

A frog's life

These photographs show the life cycle of a frog. Adult frogs lay eggs, called spawn, in ponds. The eggs hatch into tadpoles. Over several weeks a tadpole's tail shrinks, it grows legs and then turns into a frog.

Science explained

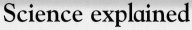

Butterflies lay eggs on leaves. Caterpillars hatch from the eggs, feed and grow. After a few weeks, the caterpillars hang from twigs and make a case, or chrysalis, around themselves. Inside a chrysalis, a caterpillar's body changes into a butterfly. It then hatches and spreads its wings.

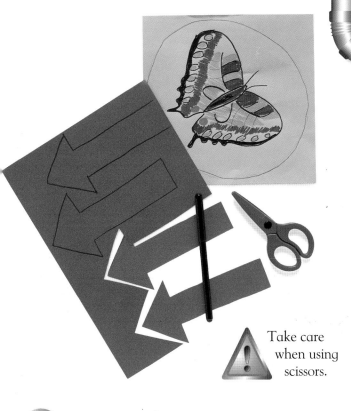

Take care when using scissors.

2 Ask an adult to help you cut out your drawings. Now draw and cut out four arrows from the card.

3 Without looking at the photographs on this page, arrange the butterfly's life cycle in the correct order using the arrows. Were you right?

37

It's quiz time!

Now that you have completed the experiments, have fun testing your knowledge of living and growing. Look back for help if you are unsure of any of the answers.

Let's go!

Can you find the odd one out?
Look at the lists of words below. Can you work out which word in each line is the odd one out?

1 legs   wings   nose   flippers

2 stripes   pebbles   spots   patches

3 stone   wood   dog   plastic cup

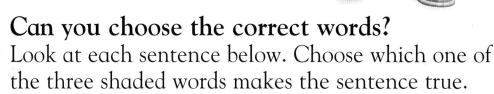
Can you choose the correct words?
Look at each sentence below. Choose which one of the three shaded words makes the sentence true.

How's it going?

1 Birds build
  (cities)   (nests)   (kennels) .

2 As you get older, your hand print will
  (shrink)   (grow)   (flatten) .

3 The middle stage in a frog's life cycle is a
  (frog)   (butterfly)   (tadpole) .

What's going on?
Can you answer the questions below?

 1 Why does Newton like eating bones?

2 What is this duckling doing?

3 Chip is nearly toppling over. Why is it easier for Newton to balance than Chip?

Now check your answers.

 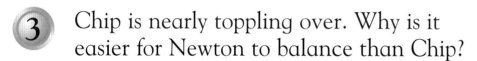 

Brilliant!!! More than 8 points

Very good!! More than 5 points

Well done! More than 3 points

Give yourself one point for each correct answer.

What's going on?
1 Newton enjoys munching on bones because he is a meat-eater.
2 The duckling is hatching, by pushing its way out of its egg.
3 Newton has four legs so it is easier for him to balance than Chip, who has only two legs.

Choose the correct words
1 Nests
2 Grow
3 Tadpole

Odd one out
1 Nose – the other words describe parts of bodies that animals use to move.
2 Pebbles – the other words are different types of camouflage.
3 Dog – the other words describe things that are not alive.

39

Your Body

Parents' notes

This section will help develop your child's understanding of the human body and how it works. Read these notes and any on the relevant pages to help your child get the most out of the experiments.

Pages 44–45: Body parts

This activity introduces your child to the different parts of the body. The activity encourages him or her to name the main external body parts and see where they join. Extend the activity by discussing what the various parts of the body are used for.

Pages 46–47: Different faces

This experiment shows your child that, although people have the same facial features, such as eyes, nose and a mouth, small differences in these features make one face look very different from another. Encourage your child to tell you what the differences are when he or she moves the mirror.

Pages 48–49: Food and drink

If your child has an allergy, make sure that you supervise his or her choice of food and drink for this activity. Discuss the advantages of eating healthy, tasty foods and the disadvantages of eating unhealthy foods. Explain to your child why it is important to eat a balanced diet.

Pages 50–51: Keeping clean

Your child should be aware of the importance of personal hygiene. Extend this activity by discussing other situations when your child needs to wash his or her hands or body. Discuss with your child why hair, teeth and nails also need regular cleaning.

Pages 52–53: Your senses

To make this test fair, the child testing his or her senses should take an equal number of sips or sniffs from each beaker. If your child's nose is blocked by a cold, he or she won't be able to name the drinks as easily. Encourage your child to think about where the different senses are located and which senses he or she has used that day, for example, hearing with ears.

Pages 54–55: How many teeth?

You will need to help your child count his or her teeth and fill in the charts. Your child may have started to develop his or her adult teeth, or may still have a full set of milk teeth. Whatever the case, your child may find it interesting to keep a record of how many milk teeth they have lost and adult teeth they have grown, by filling in the charts every six months. Use this opportunity to discuss the importance of regular teeth brushing and dental check-ups.

Pages 56–57: How you grow

Children can be sensitive about their height. The heights in this activity are average, so if your child is shorter or taller than the heights given, reassure him or her that this is not unusual. Explain to your child that some younger children can be taller than older children and vice versa.

Pages 58–59: Keeping fit

If your child has asthma, supervise any exercise required for this activity. The position of the arrows on the dials will vary depending on the exercise your child does. Encourage your child to try doing two different exercises, for example, star jumps then brisk walking, to compare the difference. For this activity to be fair, your child must rest between each exercise.

Pages 60–61: Taking medicine

This activity provides an opportunity for you to discuss the "dos" and "don'ts" surrounding medicine with your child. Make sure he or she understands why it is important to follow these rules. Some children are frightened about becoming ill and visiting a doctor, so, where appropriate, reassure your child.

Pages 62–63: Your family

Today's society is diverse and your child may not live in a typical or "nuclear" family. Explain that a family tree usually includes only relatives. If appropriate, suggest an alternative, for example, a friendship tree. Whatever the situation, encourage your child to feel positive about his or her family. If you are concerned that your child could damage the photographs, use photocopies instead.

Body parts

What does everybody have? A body, of course! Your body has lots of different parts. Each part has a special name, from the lids that cover your eyes to the toes at the end of your feet. Can you point to your chin, elbows and hips?

Now make a puppet

You will need: ★ a large piece of coloured card ★ a felt-tip pen ★ 9 paper fasteners ★ string or a large elastic band ★ a hole punch or a sharp pencil ★ scissors

1 Draw the outline of a puppet on the card. Include the main body parts: the trunk, one head, two arms, two hands, two legs and two feet.

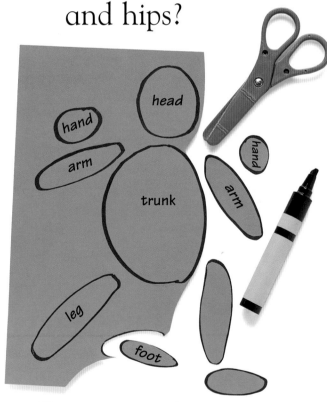

2 Now label each body part with its name. Ask an adult to help you cut out the parts.

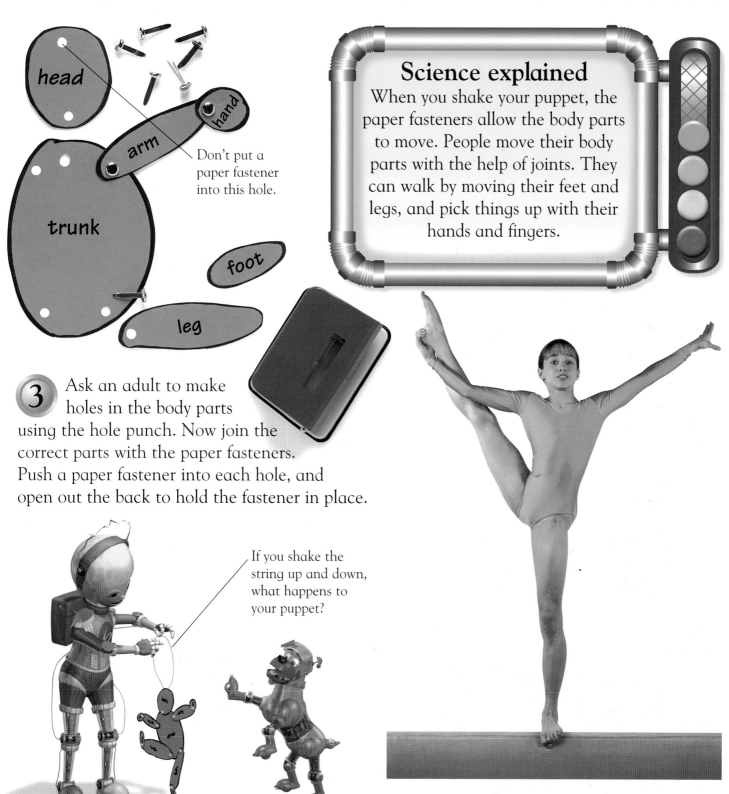

head

hand

arm

Don't put a
paper fastener
into this hole.

trunk

foot

leg

Science explained

When you shake your puppet, the paper fasteners allow the body parts to move. People move their body parts with the help of joints. They can walk by moving their feet and legs, and pick things up with their hands and fingers.

3 Ask an adult to make holes in the body parts using the hole punch. Now join the correct parts with the paper fasteners. Push a paper fastener into each hole, and open out the back to hold the fastener in place.

If you shake the string up and down, what happens to your puppet?

4 With an adult's help, thread some string through the hole in the top of the head. Make the string into a big loop and tie it at the top. Can you make your puppet dance?

Moving body

Gymnasts train their bodies so that they can move into amazing positions. This girl is using her arms, legs and feet to balance on a narrow piece of gymnastic equipment, called a beam.

45

Different faces

No two faces are exactly the same. One person may have a round face and another may have an oval face. Look at a friend's face. How is it similar to or different from yours? Are your noses the same shape and size?

Now make a changing face
You will need: ★ a large sheet of paper ★ a felt-tip pen ★ a rectangular hand mirror with a plastic edge

1. Draw the outline of a face on the sheet of paper. Draw in two eyes, a nose, a mouth and some hair around the face, as shown above.

2. Hold the mirror sideways on the paper so that it splits the face drawing in half. Now look into the mirror. What can you see?

Spot the difference

Look at the faces of these two girls. Do they look similar or different? Their expressions are different, but because they are identical twins, their faces look almost the same as each other.

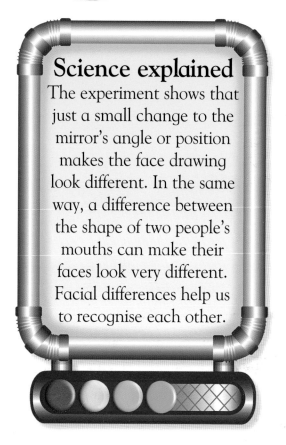

3 Now experiment by changing the mirror's angle and position on the face drawing. What happens to the face? Can you make the face drawing look wider or the eyes look closer together?

Science explained

The experiment shows that just a small change to the mirror's angle or position makes the face drawing look different. In the same way, a difference between the shape of two people's mouths can make their faces look very different. Facial differences help us to recognise each other.

Food and drink

Your body needs food and drink to keep it working properly. Food and drink give you energy, help you to grow and keep you healthy. Vegetables, rice, fish, milk and fruit are healthy and tasty foods. But watch out – lots of fatty foods, such as crisps and cakes, are not good for you.

Now make a healthy lunch
You will need: ★ a lunch box ★ 2 pieces of brown bread ★ butter or margarine ★ a round-bladed knife ★ a sandwich filling, such as cheese, lettuce and tomato ★ a chopping board ★ a sandwich bag and tie ★ a piece of fruit ★ a fruit juice drink

1 Using the knife, thinly spread some butter onto both pieces of bread.

2 Place your choice of filling on one piece of bread, and then press the other piece on top. This is your sandwich.

Science explained

This healthy lunch provides your body with the correct types of foods. The starch in the bread gives you energy to keep active, and the protein in the cheese helps you grow. Vitamins and minerals in the salad, fruit and fruit juice help your body to stay healthy.

Yum, yum!

Always wash your hands before touching or eating food.

3 Place your sandwich into a sandwich bag and tie it. Now put it into your lunch box. Add a piece of fruit, such as an apple, and a drink, such as some orange juice.

Supermarket shopping

You can buy lots of delicious, healthy foods from supermarkets and markets. On your next trip to the supermarket, look on the shelves to see how many healthy foods you can spot.

Keeping clean

Have you washed your hands today? Even if they look clean, your hands may have touched something that had invisible bugs, called germs, on it. Germs can make you ill. Washing your hands with soap and water helps get rid of germs.

Now try this activity
You will need: ★ 4 pieces of coloured card ★ a pencil ★ a felt-tip pen ★ a ruler ★ scissors

1 Ask an adult to help you cut out four cards, each about 14 cm (6 in) high by 9 cm (4 in) wide.

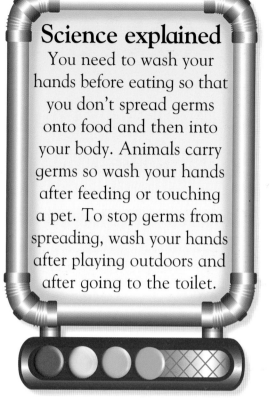

Science explained

You need to wash your hands before eating so that you don't spread germs onto food and then into your body. Animals carry germs so wash your hands after feeding or touching a pet. To stop germs from spreading, wash your hands after playing outdoors and after going to the toilet.

playing outdoors

eating a meal

feeding a pet

ACTIVITY LIST
• eating a meal
• feeding a pet
• playing outdoors
• going to the toilet

2 On each piece of card, write down one of the activities listed above.

3 Ask an adult to mix up the four activity cards. Now pick one card at a time. Look at the activity on the card and tell the adult if you would wash your hands before the activity or after it.

Bathtime fun

Your whole body needs washing to stay clean and healthy. In the bath you can wash all over with soap and warm water.

Your senses

How do you know if it's a beautiful day? You can see the blue sky, feel warm sunshine, hear birds singing, smell flowers and taste an ice cream. The five senses of sight, touch, hearing, smell and taste help us to discover the world around us.

Now try this smell and taste test

You will need: ★ 4 beakers ★ 3 different fruit-flavoured juice drinks, such as orange, strawberry and blackcurrant ★ some water ★ a scarf ★ 4 sticky labels ★ a felt-tip pen ★ a friend to help

1. Pour one fruit-flavoured drink into each beaker. Pour some water into another beaker. Write the name of each drink on a sticky label. Stick it onto the correct beaker so that you don't forget which is which!

water

orange

strawberry

blackcurrant

Science explained

Your senses of smell and taste work together so you can recognise the flavours of food and drink. Your nose picks up the smell of each fruit-flavoured juice drink. Your tongue discovers if it's sweet, sour or bitter. Water has hardly any flavour or smell.

2 Ask a friend to tie the scarf over your eyes, like a blindfold. Now ask your friend to hand you one beaker at a time.

3 First, smell the drink in each beaker, then taste it. Can you name each drink? After the test, ask your friend how many drinks you named correctly.

Senses at work

Which senses is this girl using? She is using her eyes to see the rose, her nose to smell its scent and her hand to touch it.

How many teeth?

There are differently shaped teeth in your mouth. You use your sharp front teeth to bite an apple, then your flatter back teeth to chew it. You have two different sets of teeth during your life: baby teeth and then adult teeth.

Now make these teeth charts

You will need: ★ 1 large sheet of paper
★ 3 differently coloured felt-tip pens
★ a hand mirror with
a plastic edge

Wash your hands before you count your teeth.

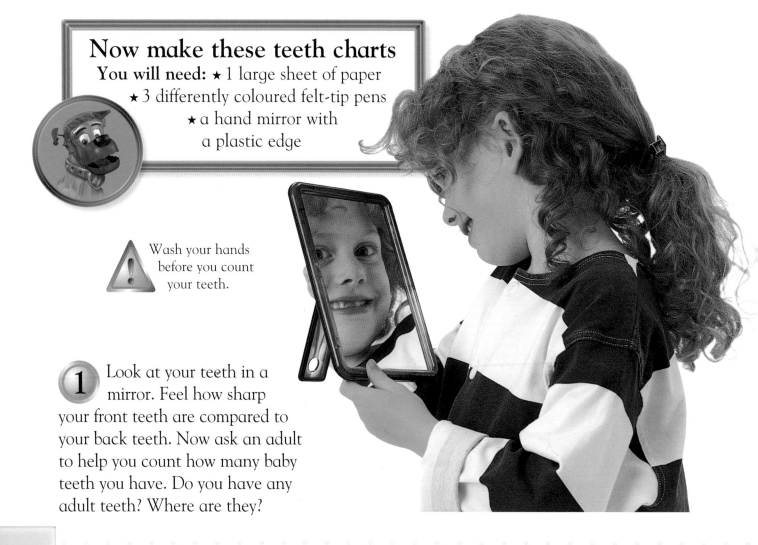

1 Look at your teeth in a mirror. Feel how sharp your front teeth are compared to your back teeth. Now ask an adult to help you count how many baby teeth you have. Do you have any adult teeth? Where are they?

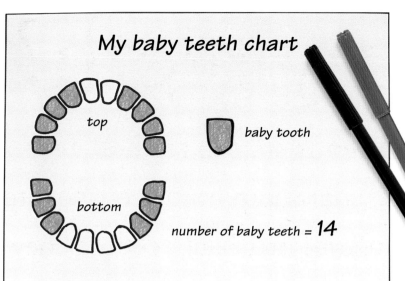

My baby teeth chart

top

baby tooth

bottom

number of baby teeth = 14

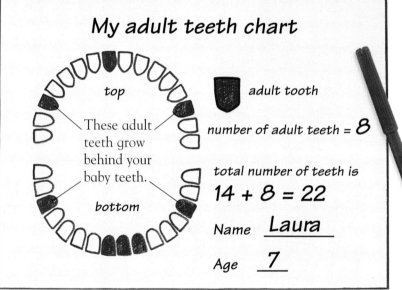

My adult teeth chart

top

These adult teeth grow behind your baby teeth.

adult tooth

number of adult teeth = 8

total number of teeth is

14 + 8 = 22

Name Laura

Age 7

bottom

2 Copy the baby teeth chart on the top half of the paper. Draw ten tooth shapes at the top and ten at the bottom. Choose a coloured pen. Now fill in where you have baby teeth. Write how many baby teeth you have.

3 Copy the adult teeth chart on the bottom half of the paper. Draw 16 tooth shapes at the top and 16 at the bottom. Choose a different coloured pen. Now fill in where you have adult teeth. Write how many adult teeth you have. To complete your charts, fill in your name and age. Finally, add up your total number of teeth.

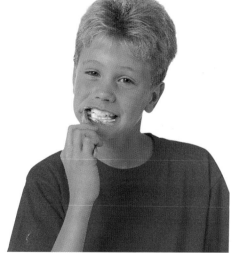

Brushing teeth

It's important to brush your teeth with toothpaste after each meal. This helps to keep your teeth clean and healthy.

Science explained

Between the ages of 6 and 12, your first 20 teeth, called baby teeth, will start to loosen and fall out, leaving gaps. These gaps will be filled by adult teeth. There are 32 teeth in a full adult set. You probably still have most of your baby teeth, but your adult teeth may have already begun to appear.

55

How you grow

Have your parents kept any of your baby clothes? You won't fit into them now! Your body has been growing since you were born. You probably won't notice how much you've grown until your trousers are too short or your shoes are too tight. Then you know you are ready for a bigger size.

Now make a height tower

You will need: ★ 7 cardboard tubes each about 24 cm (9 in) long ★ 7 pieces of coloured card each about 24 cm (9 in) long ★ a felt-tip pen ★ sticky tape ★ scissors

0 years

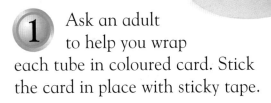

1 Ask an adult to help you wrap each tube in coloured card. Stick the card in place with sticky tape.

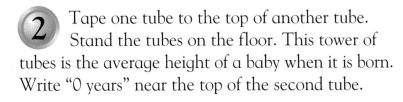

2 Tape one tube to the top of another tube. Stand the tubes on the floor. This tower of tubes is the average height of a baby when it is born. Write "0 years" near the top of the second tube.

Growing up

Can you guess the ages of these children by looking at their heights? The shortest boy is four years old, the girl in the middle is seven years old and the tallest boy is ten years old.

Stand next to the tower and look down to see how much you have grown since you were a baby.

1 year

0 years

3 Tape a third tube onto the top of the other two. The tower is now the average height of a one-year-old child. Write "1 year" near the top of the third tube.

Whooooosh!

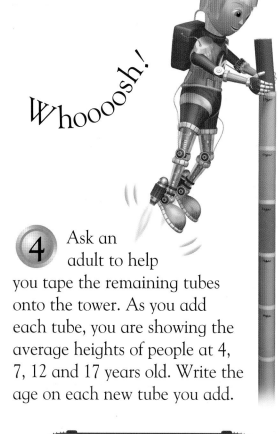

4 Ask an adult to help you tape the remaining tubes onto the tower. As you add each tube, you are showing the average heights of people at 4, 7, 12 and 17 years old. Write the age on each new tube you add.

Science explained

Not everyone is the same height at the same age. As the tower shows, children grow fastest in their first year. From then until about 12 years old, children grow steadily. For a short while teenagers grow more quickly as they change into adults, then at about 17 years old they stop growing.

Keeping fit

Do you like playing chase and catch in the park with your friends? You run, dodge, shout and laugh. Before long, your breathing quickens and you feel warm. Exercise is fun, makes you feel good and helps to keep your body healthy.

Now make this exercise meter

You will need: ★ a large piece and a small piece of coloured card ★ a felt-tip pen ★ scissors ★ 3 paper fasteners ★ a sharp pencil ★ an old CD ★ a watch or a clock with a second hand

If you have asthma, only exercise with adult supervision.

1 On the large piece of card, draw carefully around the CD three times to make three circles. These are your dials.

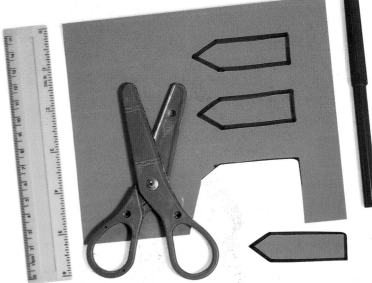

2 Now draw three arrows on the small piece of card, each about 5 cm (2 in) long by 2 cm (1 in) wide. Ask an adult to help you cut out the arrows.

58

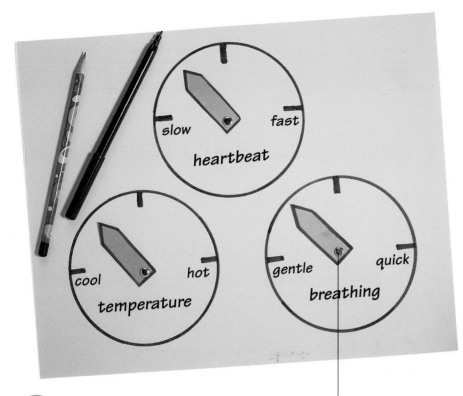

Science explained

When you are exercising, the muscles in your body work harder than when you are resting. Your heart beats faster to pump blood to your muscles. You need more air so you breathe more quickly. When you exercise, your body heats up – sweating helps to cool you down.

3 Label the dials as shown above. Ask an adult to make a hole in the middle of each dial using the sharp pencil. Use a paper fastener to attach an arrow to each dial.

Push a paper fastener through each hole, and open out the back to hold the arrow in place.

Are you breathing gently or hard? Do you feel hot or cold? Is your heart beating slow or fast?

4 Now sit quietly. Turn the arrows to show how your body feels. Then time yourself for two minutes as you do some exercise, such as ten star jumps or running around. Now move the arrows to show how you feel.

School sports day

Does your school have a sports day? Taking part in the events, such as running races, is good exercise and lots of fun. But it doesn't matter if you don't win!

Taking medicine

Sometimes people become ill. If you are ill, an adult may take you to see a doctor who may give you some medicine to make you feel better. Design a poster to help you learn the "dos" and "don'ts" of taking medicine.

Now design a poster

You will need: ★ a large sheet of paper ★ glue ★ scissors ★ felt-tip pens ★ a ruler ★ pictures of doctors, nurses, patients and medicines from pamphlets and old magazines

Taking Medicine	
Do	Don't

Make sure you leave enough space around your chart to glue your pictures.

Taking Medicine	
Do	Don't
• visit a doctor when you feel ill	• take other people's medicine
•	

1 Draw lines on your paper, as shown above. Write the title "Taking Medicine" across the top two columns. Label one column "Do" and the other column "Don't".

2 Read the "Dos" and "Don'ts" in the two columns above. Can you think of any more rules to add to your poster? Write them in the correct columns.

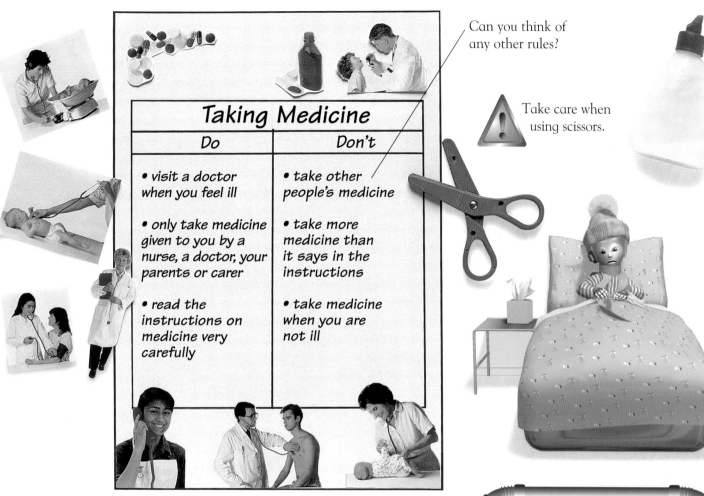

Taking Medicine

Do	Don't
• visit a doctor when you feel ill	• take other people's medicine
• only take medicine given to you by a nurse, a doctor, your parents or carer	• take more medicine than it says in the instructions
• read the instructions on medicine very carefully	• take medicine when you are not ill

Can you think of any other rules?

Take care when using scissors.

3 Cut out some pictures of doctors, nurses, patients and medicines from pamphlets and magazines. Glue the pictures around your poster. You could draw some pictures, too!

Only take medicine given to you by a nurse, a doctor, your parents or carer. Never touch other people's medicine.

Feeling ill

This girl is ill and is being given liquid medicine. This will soon make her well again.

Science explained

When you are ill, taking medicine helps your body to fight the illness so you can become well again. Do not take medicine when you are not ill because it could harm you. Taking someone else's medicine or too much medicine can be very dangerous.

Your family

All families are different. As well as parents, brothers and sisters, there are lots of people that can make up a family. You may have a half-sister or a stepfather, or aunts, cousins and grandparents. How are the people in your family related to you?

Now make a family tree
You will need: ★ a large and a small piece of coloured card ★ double-sided sticky tape ★ photographs of your family, such as grandparents, parents, brothers, sisters and yourself ★ scissors ★ a felt-tip pen

Take care when using scissors.

Your family tree may include uncles, aunts and cousins.

1 Put sticky tape behind each photograph. Stick photographs of your grandparents along the top of the large piece of card. Now stick photographs of your parents underneath. Stick photographs of you and any brothers and sisters along the bottom.

2 Cut some labels out of the small piece of card. On each label, write the name of the person in each photograph and how that person is related to you.

Family likenesses

If you look at the family above, you will see that some of the people look alike. This is because parents pass down their features to their children. Grandparents, parents, brothers, sisters, aunts, uncles and cousins can all share the same looks.

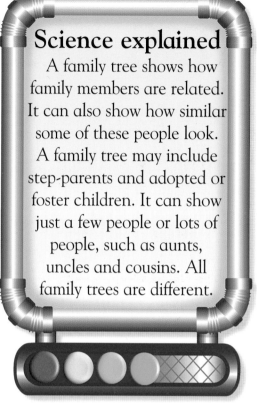

Science explained

A family tree shows how family members are related. It can also show how similar some of these people look. A family tree may include step-parents and adopted or foster children. It can show just a few people or lots of people, such as aunts, uncles and cousins. All family trees are different.

3 Use the tape to stick the labels underneath the correct photographs. Now draw lines to show how you are related to the people in the photographs.

4 Finally, look at your completed family tree. It will probably look different from this one. Do you look like any of the other people in your family that you are related to?

It's quiz time!

Now that you have completed the experiments, have fun testing your knowledge of the body. Look back for help if you are unsure of any of the answers.

Let's go!

Can you find the odd one out?
Look at the lists of words below. Can you work out which word in each line is the odd one out?

1 leg   arm   foot   string

2 smell   touch   flower   taste

3 nose   mouth   eyes   smile

Can you choose the correct words?
Look at each sentence below. Choose which one of the three shaded words makes the sentence true.

How's it going?

1 All families are
(small)   (different)   (large) .

2 Before a meal, always wash your hands with water and (soap)   (juice)   (medicine) .

3 You brush your teeth with a toothbrush and (toes)   (milk)   (toothpaste) .

What's going on?

Can you answer the questions below?

1 Why is this girl being given medicine?

2 Why is Chip breathing more quickly than usual?

3 What healthy foods are Chip and Pixel eating for their packed lunches?

Now check your answers.

Give yourself one point for each correct answer.

Well done!  More than 3 points

Very good!! 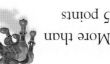 More than 5 points

Brilliant!!!  More than 8 points

What's going on?
1 This girl is being given medicine because she is ill.
2 Chip is breathing quicker than normal because he is exercising.
3 Chip and Pixel are eating brown bread and salad sandwiches. They each have a piece of fruit for dessert and fruit juice to drink.

Choose the correct words
1 Different
2 Soap
3 Toothpaste

Odd one out
1 String – the other words are names of parts of the body.
2 Flower – all the other words are names of parts of the face.
3 Smile – the other words are types of senses.

Plants

Parents' notes

This section will help your child to learn about flowering plants and to investigate what they need in order to grow. Read these notes and any on the relevant pages to help your child get the most out of the experiments.

Pages 70–71: Parts of a plant

This activity will help your child to recognise and name the parts of a flowering plant. Encourage your child to look at different plants and to name each part. Explain that all flowering plants have the same basic parts.

Pages 72–73: Green leaves

Leaves are many shapes and sizes, but they all use sunlight, air and water to make food for the rest of the plant. This activity will help your child to compare different leaves. Help your child to study leaf veins by looking at them through a magnifying glass.

Pages 74–75: Finding water

Here, your child can observe how roots grow. Discuss how all plants need water to grow and explain how they suck it up through their roots. You can explain that roots also help to anchor plants. If you have a garden, show your child the roots of any new plants you are planting or weeds you pull up.

Pages 76–77: Watering plants

This experiment demonstrates how water travels up the stem of a plant to the flowers. For the best results, add quite a lot of food colouring to the plant water and keep the flowers in a warm, bright place.

Pages 78–79: Find the light

All plants grow towards the light. This experiment shows how a stem can change the direction in which it is growing in search of sunlight. Explain to your child that flowering plants need light to grow and do not grow well in dark places.

Pages 80–81: Watch it grow

This experiment shows how a plant starts to grow from a seed. It is important that the kitchen paper remains damp. Encourage your child to look at the bean seed a couple of times a day and discuss any signs of change. Explain that this is how seeds normally start to grow under the ground.

Pages 82–83: Cress heads

Seeds need water and warmth in order to start growing well. To make this experiment fair, your child must water the three watered shells every day. Discuss with your child how best to grow flower seeds and whether they should be planted in spring, summer, autumn or winter.

Pages 84–85: Beautiful flowers

This activity will help your child to recognise and compare different flowers. Encourage your child to look carefully at different flowers, noting their shape, colour and the number of petals. Suggest to your child that he or she watches what insects do when they land on flowers.

Pages 86–87: What's inside?

Here your child is encouraged to recognise different fruits and seeds. Discuss the similarities and differences between different fruits. You will need to explain that some "vegetables" such as tomatoes and peppers have seeds inside them, and are really fruits. Warn your child not to eat fruits or seeds from wild plants as some are poisonous.

Pages 88–89: Sowing seeds

The activities on these pages will help your child to observe some of the different ways seeds are dispersed. Encourage your child to think of other types of seeds and how they are spread, for example acorns and coconuts. Explain that seeds have to be carried away from their parent plant by wind, animals or water, so that they have enough space and light to grow well.

Parts of a plant

Plants grow almost everywhere on Earth. They give us food to eat, keep the air fresh and make the world look beautiful. Without them, animals could not live. Now find out more about the different parts of a plant.

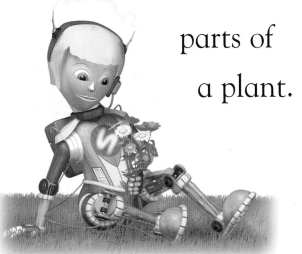

1 Look at a flowering plant. On different coloured felt, draw the different parts of the plant – some roots, a stem, leaves and petals and the centre of the flower.

Draw the leaves and stem on green felt.

2 Carefully, cut out the plant parts.

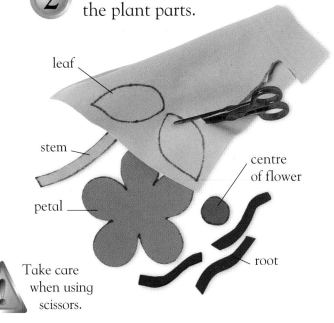

leaf

stem

petal

centre of flower

root

Take care when using scissors.

3 Arrange the parts of the plant on the card to make a picture of a flowering plant. When the parts are in the correct place, glue them onto the card.

Look at a flowering plant to help you find out where to put each part.

4 Now look at your flower picture. What do you think the different parts of the plant do?

Roots grow downwards.

The rest of the plant grows upwards.

Science explained

Most plants have the same main parts. Roots grow down into the soil in search of water. A stem holds the plant up. Green leaves spread out to catch the sunlight. The brightly coloured petals attract birds and insects to the flowers. The centre of the flower makes new seeds.

A flowering plant

Plants come in all shapes and sizes. They include tiny flowers that grow in cracks in walls, vegetables that grow in gardens and fields, and huge blossom trees like this one.

71

Green leaves

Did you know that you can recognise trees and most other plants by the shape of their leaves? Leaves come in many different shapes and sizes, but they are usually green. Take a closer look at some leaves – how many can you find that are of a different shape?

Now make some leaf prints

You will need: ★ different tree leaves ★ a paintbrush ★ coloured poster paints ★ a pen ★ sheets of newspaper ★ an apron ★ a sheet of thick paper or card ★ some water

The dull side of the leaf should face upwards.

1 Put on an apron and cover a table with newspaper. Place the leaves on the newspaper, with the shiny side of each leaf facing downwards.

2 Paint the dull underside of the leaf with a thin coat of paint mixed with a little water. Make sure you completely cover the leaf.

Falling leaves

Some trees, like this birch tree, grow new leaves each spring. In the autumn, the green leaves turn brown and fall to the ground. Other trees keep their leaves all the year round.

3 Press the painted side of the leaf firmly onto the card, then carefully peel it off.

Some leaves have jagged edges like this.

Oak tree

Cherry tree

Japanese maple tree

Gingko tree

Vine leaf

You can choose different colours for your prints.

Each print shows the shape of the leaf.

4 Make prints of the other leaves in the same way. Label each print with the name of the tree that the leaf came from. To help you label them, look up the leaves in a book on trees.

Science explained

Look closely at the leaf prints and you will see tiny lines or tubes called leaf veins. Water, gases and food run to and from the rest of the tree along these veins. Leaves use water, gases from the air and sunlight to make the food plants need to grow.

Finding water

Like you, plants need to drink water, but they drink it up through their roots. On a new plant, the roots are the first part of the plant to grow. Roots grow down into the soil where it is dark and damp.

Now watch roots grow
You will need: ★ an onion or hyacinth bulb ★ a jam jar filled with water ★ 3 cocktail sticks ★ liquid plant food ★ a teaspoon

Plant food helps plants to grow well.

Jam jar filled with water.

The bottom of the onion must touch the water.

1 Pour some liquid plant food onto a teaspoon. Add a few drops to the water.

2 Ask an adult to help you push the cocktail sticks into the onion. Rest them on the jar so the bottom of the onion touches the water.

3 Put the jar on a warm windowsill, and leave it for a few days. Can you see tiny roots growing down? Leave the onion for another few days. Now what can you see?

Green shoots sprout from the top of the onion. They will grow into stems, leaves and flowers.

You may need to top up the water to keep the bottom of the onion wet.

Science explained

The onion's roots grow down into the water. They suck up water, like tiny drinking straws. As the onion shoots sprout, it needs more water, so it grows more roots. The roots also suck up special substances called minerals. These help to keep the plant healthy.

Spreading roots

Tree roots spread out as far below the ground as the branches do above. As well as taking up water from the ground, the strong roots hold the tree firmly in place.

Watering plants

Do you know what happens to the water when you water a plant? After the roots have sucked the water up, they pass it into the plant's stem. What exactly happens to the water after that? Try this experiment to find out.

Now colour some flowers

You will need: ★ about 6 white carnations ★ a knife ★ a chopping board ★ 2 clear jars, nearly full of water ★ red and blue food colouring

Ask an adult to trim the flower stems with the knife.

Watering plants

When you water a plant, it is best to water the soil or compost around the stem. The plant's roots suck up the water, then the stem draws the water up the plant to the leaves and flowers.

It is best to cut the flower stems diagonally.

1 Lay the white carnations on the chopping board. Ask an adult to slice off the ends of the stems at the base, as shown.

2 Add about ten drops of red food colouring to one jar and about ten drops of blue food colouring to the other jar.

Science explained
The carnations suck up water through their stems into their flowers and leaves. Water and food travel around a plant inside tiny hollow tubes called veins. You can see the coloured water inside the veins in the carnations' petals.

3 Stand two or three carnations in each jar. Leave them in a warm place overnight.

The coloured water reaches the ends of the petals.

4 Now look at the flowers. What has happened to them? Look closely at the flowers' petals. Can you see tiny lines of blue or red across them?

77

Find the light

Plants need light and water to grow but they cannot get up and move from place to place, as animals can. Instead, plants find light by growing in a certain direction. Try growing a bean plant in a maze to see how it finds its way towards the sunlight.

Now make a plant maze

You will need: ★ a shoe box with a lid ★ a large piece of card ★ a pencil ★ sticky tape ★ scissors ★ a runner bean seed ★ a small plant pot filled with potting compost ★ a jug of water

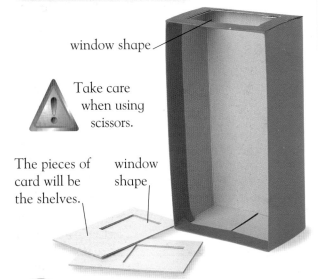

window shape

⚠ Take care when using scissors.

The pieces of card will be the shelves.

window shape

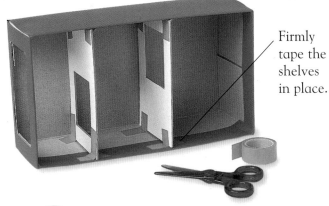

Firmly tape the shelves in place.

1 Cut a large window shape in one end of the box. Stand the box upright on the card and draw around the end of it twice. Cut out the two rectangles you have drawn. Cut a large window in each piece of card.

2 Tape one shelf into the box near one end. Tape the other shelf towards the middle of the box. Make sure the windows are not directly above each other.

3 Push the bean seed into the pot, just beneath the surface of the compost. Stand the box on its end, with the window at the top. Put the plant pot beneath the lowest window, and water the seed. Now firmly tape the lid onto the box.

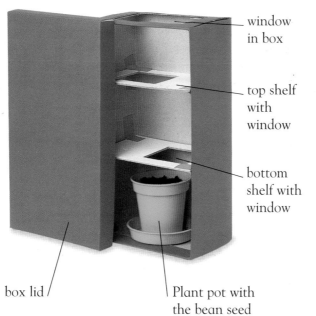

window in box

top shelf with window

bottom shelf with window

box lid

Plant pot with the bean seed planted in it.

The seedling grows towards the light.

⚠️ Always wash your hands after touching soil or compost.

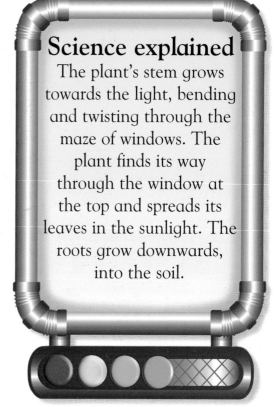

When you have checked the plant and watered it, tape the lid back on.

4 Stand the box in a warm, light place. Every few days, take off the lid to water the plant and to see how it is growing.

Towards the light
Even in a thick forest, sunlight shines through the trees. The plants and trees grow up towards the light.

Science explained
The plant's stem grows towards the light, bending and twisting through the maze of windows. The plant finds its way through the window at the top and spreads its leaves in the sunlight. The roots grow downwards, into the soil.

Watch it grow

All living things, including plants, reproduce. Many plants reproduce by making seeds from which new plants grow. If you plant a seed in a warm, damp place, it will soon sprout roots and a shoot. Eventually, the seed should grow into a healthy plant.

Now watch a plant grow
You will need: ★ a runner bean seed ★ a sheet of kitchen paper ★ a jam jar ★ a round-bladed knife ★ a jug of water

The kitchen paper soaks up the water.

The bean swells as it takes in water.

A tiny rootlet grows downwards.

1 Fold the kitchen paper in half, then roll it into a narrow tube, and slide it into the jar.

2 With the knife, push the seed between the paper and the jar. Pour a little water into the jar to wet the paper.

3 Look at the bean every day. Can you see it swell? As its outer skin splits, a root appears and starts to grow.

From seed to tree

It's hard to believe, but this huge tree, called a giant redwood tree, first grew from a tiny seed. It can take hundreds of years for a tree to grow this tall. They can grow to over 111 metres (364 ft) – that's as tall as 63 adults standing one on top of another!

Science explained

A seed stores just enough food to start a new plant. When the root and shoot first sprout from a seed they use the food in the seed to grow. This is why the seed can grow without soil. To grow into a strong, healthy plant, the seed must be planted in soil, in a light place.

shoot uncurling

runner bean seed

Rootlets growing out from the root.

Always wash your hands after touching seeds or soil.

4 If the paper looks dry, add some more water. Watch as the root grows bigger and tiny rootlets grow out from it. At the same time, a small shoot uncurls and starts to grow upwards. Soon, the shoot will grow into a stem and produce leaves.

5 When your bean plant is too big for the jar, plant it in a pot, or out in the garden, like Pixel is doing. When it is fully grown, the plant will produce flowers and then runner beans with more bean seeds inside.

Cress heads

Where do plants grow? The answer is nearly everywhere on Earth. There are only a few places where plants cannot grow, such as deep, dark caves or very cold places. Try growing some seeds in different places to find out what plants need to grow well.

Now find out more
You will need: ★ cress, mustard or alfalfa seeds ★ 4 empty eggshells ★ cotton wool ★ 4 egg cups ★ a round-bladed knife ★ felt-tip pens ★ a teaspoon ★ water

Desert flowers
Seeds in hot, dry deserts do not grow most of the time. But if it rains, they quickly burst into flower, and make new seeds before they die.

1 Cut off the tops of four boiled eggs. Scoop out the middles. Stand the shells in the egg cups, then draw funny faces on them.

cress seeds on top of the cotton wool

packet of seeds

2 Fill each eggshell with cotton wool. Sprinkle several seeds on top of the cotton wool in each shell. Try to sprinkle the seeds evenly and thinly all over the cotton wool.

3 Add a teaspoon of water to three of the shells. Leave the fourth one dry. Put one watered shell and the dry shell on a warm, light windowsill. Put one watered shell in a warm, dark cupboard and one in the fridge.

4 Every day, add more water to three of the shells but leave the fourth one dry. Check them all to see how the seeds are growing. Which seeds are growing best?

Wash your hands after touching the seeds.

Watered seeds put in a dark cupboard.

Watered seeds put in a fridge.

Seeds that weren't watered and put on a windowsill.

Seeds placed on a warm, sunny windowsill.

Beautiful flowers

How many different flowers can you see if you look in a garden or a park? Flowers are colourful and come in many different shapes and sizes. Flowers are for everyone to enjoy, so remember only to pick flowers with an adult's permission, and never pick wild flowers.

1 Open a big book and lay two sheets of kitchen paper on it. Arrange the flowers flat on one sheet of paper.

Now press some flowers
You will need: ★ garden flowers ★ big, heavy books ★ several sheets of kitchen paper ★ glue ★ a piece of card ★ a hole punch ★ sticky film ★ ribbon

2 Close the page. Press some more flowers in the same way on another page. Close the book, and stack some heavy books on top of it.

3 After about four weeks, take out the pressed flowers. To make a picture or card, dab a tiny spot of glue on the back of each flower and gently stick it in place on the piece of card.

4 Use as many differently shaped and coloured flowers as you can to complete your card. You can also make a bookmark by gluing dried flowers onto a strip of card.

To make the bookmark stronger, cover it with sticky film.

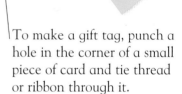

To make a gift tag, punch a hole in the corner of a small piece of card and tie thread or ribbon through it.

Drinking from a flower

This flower is the perfect shape for a hummingbird to drink from. The bird puts its beak inside the flower to drink its sweet-tasting liquid, called nectar.

Science explained

On the card, you can see the shapes and colours of the flowers that attract insects and birds. A powder inside each flower, called pollen, sticks to the insects and birds. When they land on a new flower, the pollen brushes off. This helps the flower to make new seeds.

What's inside?

What is your favourite fruit? Bananas, grapes, strawberries or watermelon? The fruit is the part of a plant that surrounds the seeds. The fruit we eat is usually sweet, soft and juicy, but what is inside it? Read on to find out.

Ask an adult to cut the fruit.

Now look inside fruits

You will need: ★ a selection of fruits ★ a knife ★ a teaspoon ★ a saucer ★ felt-tip pens ★ a sheet of paper ★ a chopping board

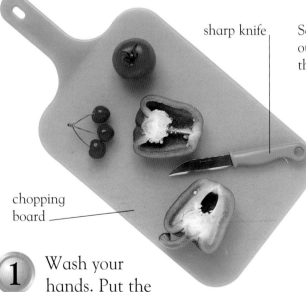

sharp knife

chopping board

Scoop the seeds out of one half of the green pepper.

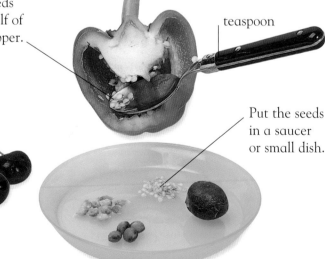

teaspoon

Put the seeds in a saucer or small dish.

1 Wash your hands. Put the different fruits on the chopping board. Ask an adult to cut each one in half with the knife.

2 Use the spoon to scoop out the seeds from one half of each fruit. How many seeds are there in each one?

Science explained

A soft fruit grows around the seeds of some flowering plants to protect the seeds. Some fruits have lots of seeds and others contain just one big seed, called a stone. The seeds in a fruit are often called pips. Animals and birds eat the juicy fruit and help to spread its seeds.

3 Look at the other half of each fruit. Does each one also have seeds or stones? Now draw a picture of these halves.

4 Colour in the pictures. Write labels around each part of your drawings, showing the different parts of the fruits, such as the skin, seeds and flesh.

Tasty seeds

Did you know that coconuts are giant seeds? They grow inside large fruits on palm trees. The white flesh and watery milk inside coconut shells are good to eat.

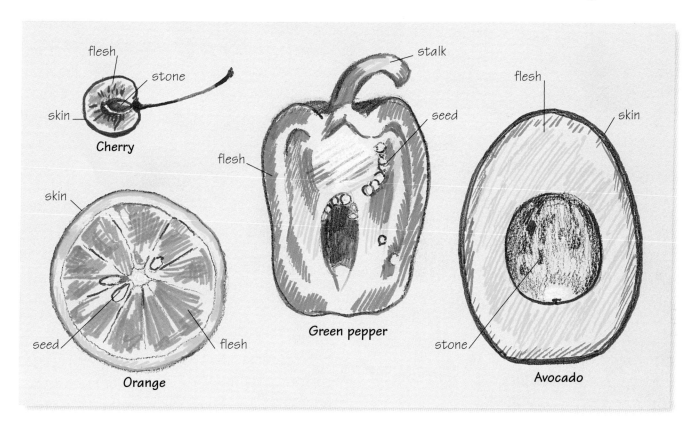

flesh
stone
skin
Cherry

stalk
seed
flesh
Green pepper

flesh
skin
stone
Avocado

skin
seed
flesh
Orange

87

Sowing seeds

Peanuts, broad beans, peas, sesame seeds, grass seeds and acorns are all different seeds. How do they spread from the plants that made them to places where they have room to grow? To find out, look for as many types of seeds as you can during the summer and autumn.

Make sure an adult is nearby when you stand on the chair.

Now sow some seeds
You will need: ★ a pea pod ★ winged tree seeds ★ burrs ★ a parachute seed head ★ a magnifying glass ★ a chair

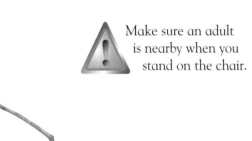

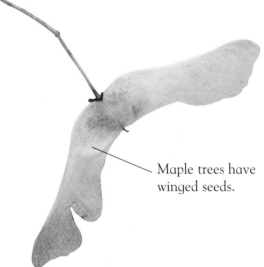

Maple trees have winged seeds.

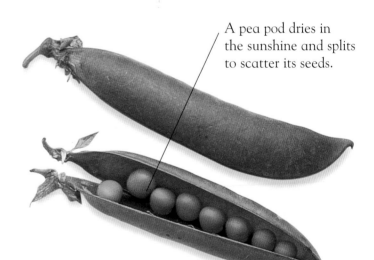

A pea pod dries in the sunshine and splits to scatter its seeds.

1 Carefully stand on a chair, and drop the winged tree seeds from a height. Watch how they spin like helicopters as they fall.

2 Split open a pea pod and push out the peas. See how far the peas scatter around you.

3 Now hold a fluffy parachute seed head in front of you and blow hard. Watch how the tiny seeds take off and float away on the breeze.

Each seed has its own miniature parachute.

A burr is covered with tiny hooks.

4 Now look closely at the burrs with the magnifying glass. Can you see why they stick to your clothes and animals' fur?

Science explained

Winged seeds and parachute seeds are carried away by the wind. The wind blows seed pod heads, shaking the seeds out. Some seeds float to new places along streams and rivers. Burrs catch on the fur or feathers of passing animals. After a while, the seeds drop to the ground.

Spreading seeds

This young gorilla likes to eat juicy fruit. As he eats the fruit, seeds drop onto the ground. Some of the seeds will grow into new plants.

It's quiz time!

Now that you have completed the experiments, have fun testing your knowledge of plants. Look back for help if you are unsure of any of the answers.

Let's go!

Can you find the odd one out?
Look at the lists of words below. Can you work out which word in each line is the odd one out?

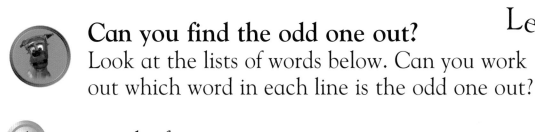

1 stem   leaf   eye   root

2 strawberry   orange   flower   banana

3 conker   acorn   sunlight   peanut

Can you choose the correct words?
Look at each sentence below. Choose which one of the three shaded words makes the sentence true.

How's it going?

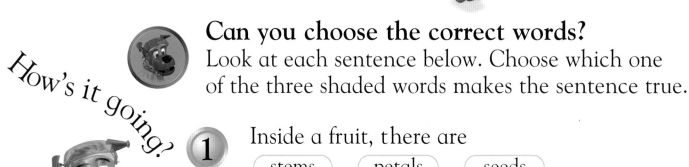

1 Inside a fruit, there are
  stems   petals   seeds .

2 A plant grows towards the
  door   sunlight   wind .

3 The first parts of a plant to grow are the
  roots   leaves   flowers .

What's going on?

Can you answer the questions below?

1 Pixel can name the main parts of a flowering plant. Can you?

2 Chip is looking at a leaf through a magnifying glass. What can he see?

3 What is the best part of a plant for Newton to water?

Now check your answers.

Give yourself one point for each correct answer.

 **Well done!**
More than **3 points**

 **Very good!!**
More than **5 points**

 **Brilliant!!!**
More than **8 points**

Odd one out

1 Eye – the other words are all parts of a plant.

2 Flower – the other words are all kinds of fruit.

3 Sunlight – all the other words are examples of seeds.

Choose the correct words

1 Seeds

2 Sunlight

3 Roots

What's going on?

1 The main parts of a flowering plant are the roots, stem, leaves, flower, centre and petals.

2 Chip can see the leaf veins inside the leaf.

3 Newton should water the soil or compost around the stem, so that the plant's roots can suck up the water.

Exploring Nature

Parents' notes

This section will help your child to learn more about plants and animals by exploring nature. Read these notes and any on the relevant pages to help your child get the most out of the experiments.

Pages 96–97: Nature notes

Using a nature notebook helps your child to observe and learn about the different kinds of plants and animals in the local environment. Encourage your child to take the notebook with you whenever you visit a park or go on a walk, and help him or her to record details of any interesting wildlife.

Pages 98–99: A collection

Making a collection encourages your child to examine natural objects more closely. Your child could collect objects with a theme, such as tree seeds and cones, objects from the beach, or bird feathers. Help your child to look up the objects he or she finds in reference books to identify exactly what they are.

Pages 100–101: Minibeasts

This activity draws your child's attention to the small creatures in the world around us. Explain to your child that you must always return a minibeast safely to the place where you found it and be careful not to damage its home.

Pages 102–103: Animal groups

Here your child learns to group animals according to observable similarities. Your child's "pairs" do not have to belong to the same animal group – they could just share a characteristic. For example, an eagle and a dog could both be classified as animals that eat meat.

Pages 104–105: Garden birds

For safety reasons, an adult needs to cut the holes in the plastic bottle to make this bird feeder. Encourage your child to observe which types of birds use the feeder, and which don't. Extend the activity by discussing how birds' beaks are suited to the particular food that they eat.

Pages 106–107: Pond life

This pond viewer allows your child to look under the surface of a pond or stream to see what creatures live there. To use the viewer, your child will need to be quite close to the water's surface, so strict adult supervision is necessary.

Pages 108–109: A place to live

This activity encourages your child to identify animal habitats and to think about how animals are suited to the place in which they live. Discuss with your child which characteristics of the animals on his or her poster help them to live in their habitat.

Pages 110–111: Garden life

Making and observing a bottle garden will show your child the importance of plants in the environment. Explain how the plants create and maintain their own environment in the bottle, taking water from the soil and releasing it through their leaves, recycling gases from the air and using sunlight to make their own food.

Pages 112–113: Nature at home

This activity teaches your child about the different needs of plants and animals. Explain to your child that although plants do not have feelings like animals and do not need exercise or company, they still have needs. Plants cannot survive without soil, water and light.

Pages 114–115: Caring for nature

Playing this game will teach your child how things that we do in our everyday lives can help or harm the environment. Talk to your child about some simple things that he or she could do – or stop doing – to help nature. This could be switching off lights, walking to school instead of going by car, or taking things to the local recycling centre. Encourage your child to think of other ways of caring for nature.

Nature notes

Look around you. Before long, you will probably see different plants and animals. Wherever you live, in the country or the city, there will be plenty of animals and plants to discover and study.

Take care when using scissors.

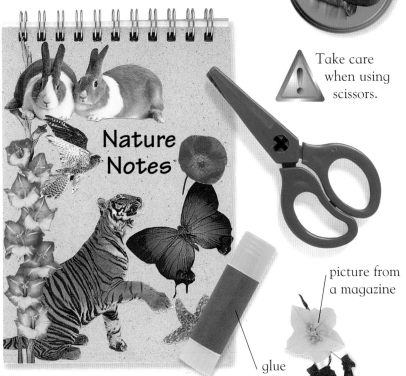

Nature Notes

picture from a magazine

glue

Slug

Date: 24th April
Time: midday
Where: in the flowerbed, eating a leaf
Description: black and slimy
Size: 7 cm (3 in)
Weather: warm and wet

1 Label the cover of your notebook "Nature Notes". Cut out some pictures of plants and animals from magazines and stick them on the cover.

2 When you see an interesting animal or plant, draw a picture of it in your notebook. Write down when and where you saw it and any other details, such as its colour and size.

Science explained

Even in the busiest city, animals and plants manage to find a place to live. Pigeons huddle together on windowsills, and blackbirds make nests in trees. There may even be ducks in the park. Recording what you see in your notebook will help you to understand living things better.

Feeding wildlife

When you go to the park, take some bread to feed the birds. You will see them clearly as they swim nearer.

Make sure an adult is with you if you are near water.

3 A magnifying glass will help you to study the plants and small animals more closely.

4 If you have a camera, take pictures of the plants and animals you see. Stick the photographs in your notebook. Binoculars will help you to see birds more clearly without disturbing them.

A collection

Have you ever picked up empty shells on the beach, collected pine cones from under a tree, or found an empty snakeskin at the side of a path? Remember, it is important not to collect any living animals, birds' eggs or wild flowers.

Now make a box of treasures
You will need: ★ a cardboard box lid ★ some card ★ a ruler ★ scissors ★ double-sided sticky tape ★ cotton wool ★ a pen ★ a collection of natural things, such as seeds, cones, bird feathers, fossils or shells

⚠ Check with an adult before you touch anything that you find.

strip of card

Stick the fold to the side of the box with double-sided tape.

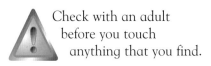
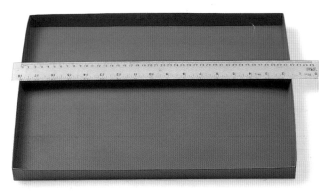

1 Measure the width of the box. Cut a strip of card about 3 cm (1 in) wide and 3 cm (1 in) longer than the box width.

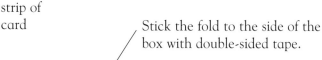

2 Make a 1.5 cm (½ in) fold at each end of the strip of card. Tape these folds to the sides of the box.

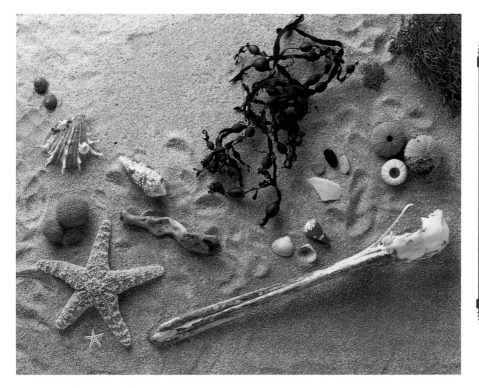

Beachcombing

Lots of natural treasures are left on the beach when the tide goes out. Here, you may find shells, starfish or seaweed.

Take care when using scissors.

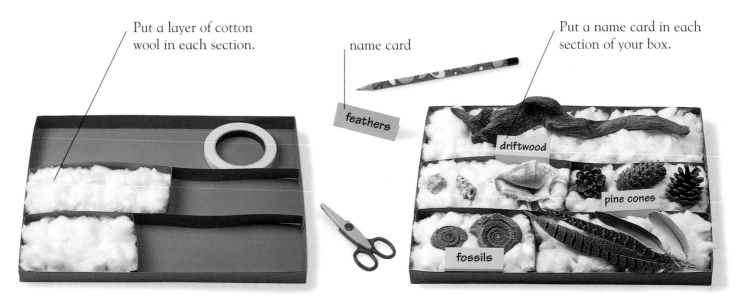

Put a layer of cotton wool in each section.

name card

Put a name card in each section of your box.

feathers

driftwood

pine cones

fossils

3 Cut out and stick on more strips of card to divide the box into sections.

4 Arrange your collection of natural items in the box. Write a name card for each item, and put the name cards in the sections.

Minibeasts

Flies, worms, spiders, bees, snails – most of the animals in the world are much smaller than we are! We call these small animals minibeasts. Minibeasts live everywhere. You can find them in the soil, on plants, under stones and in our homes.

Now try turning stones
You will need: ★ a magnifying glass ★ your nature notebook ★ a pen ★ a stick

spider with eight legs

snail with no legs (pictured), worm or slug

woodlouse with 14 legs

worm

2 Use the pictures on this page to help you identify any minibeasts you see by the number of legs they have. Do not touch the minibeasts.

centipede with lots of legs (pictured), or millipede

beetle with six legs (pictured), ant or other insect

1 Go for a walk in the park or countryside with an adult. As you walk, carefully turn over stones and fallen branches with a stick. What minibeasts can you find underneath?

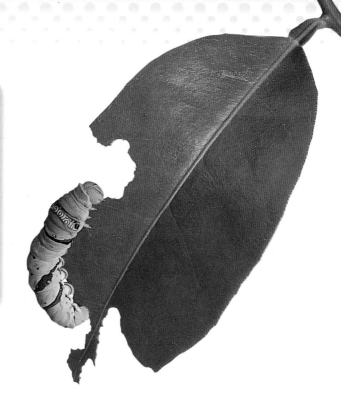

Caterpillar

You will find lots of minibeasts living on plants. This caterpillar is the young stage of a butterfly. Butterflies are insects.

⚠ Be careful not to disturb or harm the minibeasts or their homes.

worm's tail

3 Use your magnifying glass to look at each minibeast more closely. The magnifying glass lets you see more details of the minibeast.

4 In your notebook, make a note of the minibeasts you discover. Record other details, such as what a minibeast was eating.

Animal groups

Animals come in all shapes and sizes, from tiny insects you can only just see, to whales as big as buses. Some have legs, some have fins and some have wings. To keep track of all the different kinds of animals, scientists sort them into groups.

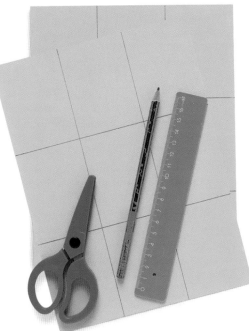

Ways of grouping animals

Has fur
Has feathers
Has six legs
Has scales and fins
Eats meat
Eats plants
Comes out at night

If you can't find pictures, you could draw animals on your cards.

Cat

Has fur

Dog

Write the name of the group under your picture.

Has fur

Take care when using scissors.

1 Ask an adult to mark out 14 cards, about 8 cm (3 in) by 5 cm (2 in) in size. Now carefully cut out the cards.

2 Choose a group from the above list, such as animals that have fur. Glue pictures of two different furry animals on two of the cards. Glue pictures of animals from another group on two more cards. Complete all the cards in the same way, making a pair of animals for each group.

Science explained

Animals with fur are mammals; animals with feathers are birds; those with scales and fins are fish and animals with six legs are insects. Meat-eating animals are carnivores and plant-eating animals are herbivores. Animals that appear at night are nocturnal animals.

Animals called mammals

Sheep belong to the animal group called mammals. Mammals have warm bodies, hair and feed their young with milk. Humans are also mammals.

Stick wrapping paper on the back of your cards.

Cat

Has fur

Dog

Has fur

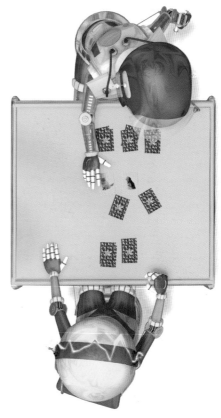

3 Now spread all the cards face down on a table. With your friend, take turns turning over two of the cards. If they make a pair, you can keep them. If they are not a pair, turn the cards over again.

4 The game is over when all the pairs have been collected. The winner is the person with the most pairs.

103

Garden birds

Birds are beautiful. Their colourful feathers and musical songs brighten up gardens and parks. Best of all, they can fly! How many different birds can you name?

Can you tell the difference between a sparrow and a robin?

Now make a bird feeder

You will need: ★ an empty, plastic water bottle with a lid ★ string ★ a short length of dowel or garden cane ★ a sharp knife ★ some wild bird food or unsalted peanuts ★ your nature notebook ★ a pen

Thread some string through the top holes.

Make sure that an adult does any cutting.

Push the stick through the bottom holes to make the perch.

Tie the ends of the string to make a loop.

feeding slit

1 Ask an adult to make two holes with the knife near the bottom of the bottle for the perch and two holes near the top of the bottle for the string hanger.

2 Now ask the adult to cut four feeding slits next to the perch. These should be about 3 cm (1 in) tall by 4 mm (⅛ in) wide.

Screw the lid on the bottle.

3 Fill the feeder with wild bird food. Hang it from a strong branch or a nail in a fence or wall.

Hang your feeder where you can see it.

4 Now sit quietly and watch the birds come to your feeder. You could use a bird guide to help you identify the different birds. Make notes and drawings in your notebook showing the birds that visit.

Science explained
The birds that visit your feeder are seed-eaters. They have strong pointed beaks for cracking shells and pecking at the seeds inside. Other birds eat different foods. Blackbirds pull up worms and starlings steal food from other birds.

Garden in winter
Birds need feeding in winter when food is difficult to find. Don't forget to put out some water for them, too.

Pond life

Is there a pond or a stream near to where you live?
Even a small garden pond will attract lots of wildlife.
Birds come to drink, and frogs will lay their eggs in the
water. Insects called
water-boatmen swim
on top of the water,
using their legs like oars.

Now make a pond viewer
You will need: ★ a 50 cm (20 in) length of
wide, plastic tubing or a large, plastic bottle
★ a sheet of clear plastic ★ scissors ★ double-
sided sticky tape ★ waterproof tape
★ your nature notebook

Underwater world
Under the water's surface, a pond is full of life.
Plants grow towards the light, frogspawn hatch
into tadpoles, and fish, newts and water
insects feed and lay eggs.

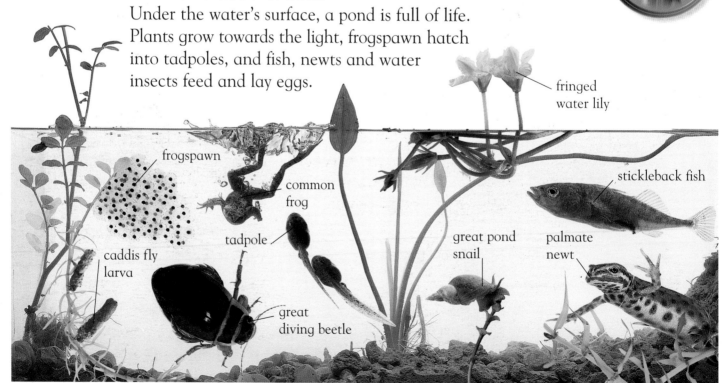

frogspawn

common
frog

fringed
water lily

stickleback fish

tadpole

caddis fly
larva

great
diving beetle

great pond
snail

palmate
newt

1 Stick a ring of double-sided tape around one end of the tube. Stretch the plastic tight over the end of the tube and stick it to the tape.

double-sided tape

clear plastic

Take care when using scissors.

2 Ask an adult to help you trim off any excess plastic around the sides of the tube with the scissors.

Make sure the plastic is tight.

3 Stick a strip of waterproof tape around the bottom of the plastic covering. This is now your pond viewer.

Waterproof tape makes sure the pond viewer doesn't leak.

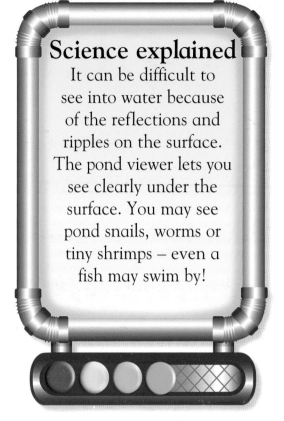

Science explained

It can be difficult to see into water because of the reflections and ripples on the surface. The pond viewer lets you see clearly under the surface. You may see pond snails, worms or tiny shrimps – even a fish may swim by!

Make sure an adult is with you when you are near the water.

4 Push the covered end of the pond viewer under the water in a pond or stream. Look down through the other end. Record your findings in your notebook.

A place to live

You won't meet a polar bear in the desert or a camel at the North Pole! It would be too hot for the polar bear and too cold for the camel. The special place where an animal likes to live is called its habitat.

Now make a habitat poster
You will need: ★ a large sheet of paper ★ a pencil ★ a ruler ★ felt-tip pens ★ magazines or books with animal pictures ★ non-toxic glue ★ scissors ★ tracing paper

Emperor penguins
Emperor penguins live in Antarctica where it is much too cold for most animals. They have lots of fat and thick coats of soft feathers to keep them warm.

Desert　Jungle

Write the name of the habitat in each section.

Draw lines with a pencil and ruler to divide the paper up.

1 Divide the paper into four sections. In each section draw a different animal habitat. It could be a desert, a jungle, the sea, the Arctic, a pond, a forest or a tree.

Take care when using scissors.

Desert　Jungle

Arctic　Sea

2 Find some pictures of animals in magazines and cut them out. You could trace pictures of animals from books, colour them in and cut them out.

3 Stick the animal pictures under the correct habitats on your poster. Can you name all the animals? Why do you think the animals you have chosen are suited to their habitats?

109

Garden life

A beautiful garden is filled with plants. The plants aren't just pretty – they are useful too. Plants keep the air fresh and provide food and homes for insects, birds and other animals.

Now make a bottle garden

You will need: ★ an old spoon ★ a stick or piece of garden cane ★ sticky tape ★ a large, clear, plastic storage jar with a lid ★ potting compost ★ small stones ★ some small plants ★ a cup ★ water ★ scissors

potting compost

jar

1 Ask an adult to tape the spoon to the stick to make a garden tool.

⚠ Always wash your hands after touching soil, or wear gloves.

tape

spoon

stick

2 Fill the bottom of the jar with stones and a layer of potting compost 5–7 cm (2–3 in) deep.

stones

Food from plants

This butterfly is feeding on juice from a bramble berry. Many animals feed on plants to live.

Once the lid is on, you won't need to water your garden again.

garden tool

small plant

Cover all the roots with soil.

cup of water

3 Using your garden tool, dig a hole in the soil. Take one of your plants out of its pot and put it in the hole. Then pack soil around the plant's roots. Plant the other plants in the same way.

4 Water your garden with a cup of water, then screw the lid on the jar. Stand your garden in a warm, sunny place. Watch the plants grow.

Nature at home

Do you keep pets or plants in your home? Are they healthy? We must treat living things with care or they will become ill, and may die. Plants and animals have different needs. Do you know how to look after both?

Decorate the edges of your chart with stickers or drawings.

If you can't find pictures, you could draw the dog and plant.

Now make this chart
You will need: ★ 2 pieces of coloured card ★ a pencil ★ a ruler ★ scissors ★ non-toxic glue ★ picture of a dog and a house plant ★ some stickers

give me food and water everyday.

put me in a bigger pot when I have grown.

water my soil.

play with me.

take me for walks.

stand me in the light.

give me a bath.

take me to a vet when I'm ill.

Cut off dead leaves and flowers.

brush my coat.

⚠ Take care when using scissors.

① Divide one piece of card into two columns. Glue the pictures of the dog and plant on the chart. Write "To take care of me you must" under each picture.

② Cut out ten strips of card from the other piece. Then write the words shown above on the strips of card.

To take care of me you must

give me food and water everyday.

To take care of me you must

stand me in the light.

take me for walks.

put me in a bigger pot when I have grown.

take me to a vet when I'm ill.

brush my coat.

give me a bath.

3 Choose one of the card strips. Decide if it should go in the column for the dog or the plant. Check if you are correct before gluing it in place.

4 Glue the other card strips in place in the same way. You could display the finished chart on a wall.

Caring for a garden

Gardeners have to look after their plants. They water them, feed them with food called fertiliser, and cut off any dead leaves and flowers.

Science explained

To stay healthy, pets need food, water and exercise. You must keep pets clean, and play with them so they don't get lonely. A plant needs damp soil for its roots to spread and to suck up water. Stand it in a warm, light place so that its leaves can make food from the sunlight.

Caring for nature

It's easy for people to spoil nature. Litter kills wild animals – they can choke on plastic bags or get tangled in old rope. Oil can kill the animals in a river or the sea. Smoke from factories and cars can make the air dirty. We should do all we can to look after nature.

Now play a nature game
You will need: ★ some small stones or buttons ★ non-toxic paints ★ paintbrushes ★ a dice ★ friends to play with

Planting trees
One way we can help nature is to plant new trees. These trees help keep the air fresh. They will grow into homes for birds and other animals.

1. Paint your stones in different colours to make game counters. You will need a counter for each person playing the game.

| 1 Start | 2 | 3 Drop sweet wrapper. Back to Start. | 4 | 5 Put sweet wrapper in bin. Forward 1. | 6 |

| 18 | 19 | 20 Reuse paper. Forward 2. | 21 Throw away a bottle. Miss a turn. | 22 | 7 Save cans for recycling. Forward 2. |

| 17 Collect silver paper. Forward 1. | 28 Drop plastic bag in pond. Miss 2 turns. | 29 | 30 Finish | 23 Leave tap running. Back 1. | 8 Walk to school. Throw again. |

| 16 Help plant a tree. Forward 3. | 27 | 26 Leave electric lights on. Back 4. | 25 Collect paper for recycling. Forward 2. | 24 | 9 |

| 15 Go by car instead of walking. Back 4. | 14 | 13 | 12 Save bottles for recycling. Forward 2. | 11 | 10 Reuse a plastic bag. Forward 3. |

2 Place your counters on the above "Start" square. Take it in turns to roll the dice and move your counter. Follow the instructions on the squares where you land. The winner is the first person to reach the "Finish" square, but you must throw the exact number to land on this square. If the number is too big, stay where you are until your next turn.

Science explained
We can help nature by reusing things again instead of throwing them away. This is called recycling. Recycling things and putting litter in bins helps nature and keeps the world looking clean and tidy. Walking instead of going by car helps to keep the air clean for animals and plants.

It's quiz time!

Now that you have completed the experiments, have fun testing your knowledge of nature. Look back for help if you are unsure of any of the answers.

Let's go!

Can you find the odd one out?
Look at the lists of words below. Can you work out which word in each line is the odd one out?

1 insect   bird   minibeast   pond

2 ladybird   bee   whale   snail

3 desert   television   jungle   Arctic

Can you choose the correct words?
Look at each sentence below. Choose which one of the three shaded words makes the sentence true.

How's it going?

1 The place where an animal lives is called its
(garden)   (group)   (habitat) .

2 When things are used again, this is called
(recycling)   (walking)   (planting) .

3 If your pet dog is ill, you would take it to a
(jungle)   (vet)   (pond) .

What's going on?
Can you answer the questions below?

 1 Chip is looking through a pond viewer. Why?

2 Why is Pixel using binoculars to watch birds?

3 How does putting your litter in a bin help wild animals?

Now check your answers.

Give yourself one point for each correct answer.

Well done! More than 3 points

Very good!! More than 5 points

Brilliant!!! More than 8 points

What's going on?
1 Chip is looking through the pond viewer because it lets him see nature below the surface of the water.
2 The binoculars allow Pixel to see the birds clearly without disturbing them.
3 Litter can kill wild animals if they eat it or get trapped in it. Putting litter in a bin is a safe way to get rid of it.

Choose the correct words
1 Habitat
2 Recycling
3 Vet

Odd one out
1 Pond – all the other words describe types of animal groups.
2 Whale – all the other words are names of minibeasts.
3 Television – all the other words describe animal habitats.

117

Glossary

Animal
An animal is a living thing that breathes and moves about. Fish, birds and reptiles are all types of animals.

Antenna
An antenna is a feeler that helps an animal to find its way around. Some animals use their antennae to smell things, in the same way that we use our noses. Antennae is the plural of antenna.

Bird
A bird is an animal that has a warm body and is covered with feathers. All birds lay eggs and many birds can fly.

Body
Every person has a body. Your body is made up of lots of different parts. The main parts of the body are the head, arms, hands, trunk, legs and feet.

Bugs
Bugs is another name for germs. Bugs is also another name for insects.

Camouflage
A camouflage is a disguise. It is made up of colours and markings that hide an animal against a background.

Carnivore
A carnivore is an animal that eats only meat. Carnivore is the opposite of herbivore.

Caterpillar
A caterpillar is the stage in a butterfly's life after it has hatched from an egg. A caterpillar spends its time feeding and it grows quickly.

Chrysalis
A chrysalis is a case that grows around a caterpillar. Inside the chrysalis, the caterpillar's body changes into a butterfly.

Egg
An egg is a round object laid by a female bird, reptile, fish or other animal. The baby animals hatch out from the eggs.

Energy

Energy makes things go. Your body needs energy to move and grow. Your body gets the energy it needs from food and drink.

Environment

The environment is the world around us where plants, animals and people live.

Exercise

Exercise means to work the muscles in your body harder than usual, such as when you are swimming or running. Exercise helps to keep your body fit and healthy.

Face

Every person has a face. The main parts of the face are two eyes, two ears, a nose, a mouth and hair. Every face is different.

Family

Your family is the people you are related to and the people you live with. Families can be large or small. Every family is different.

Family tree

A family tree is a chart that shows how the people in your family are related to one another.

Fish

A fish is an animal with bones and a cold body. It lives in water. Fish breathe with gills and swim with fins.

Flower

A flower is the part of a plant that makes seeds. Many flowers are sweetly scented and brightly coloured to attract insects and birds.

Fruit

This is the part of a plant that contains the seeds. Fruits come in many shapes and sizes. Many of them are sweet, juicy and good to eat.

Germs

Germs are invisible bugs. If germs get inside your body they can make you ill. For example, colds are caused by germs.

Habitat

This is the special place where an animal makes its home. A fish's habitat is water.

Hatch

This happens when a baby animal, such as a bird or lizard, breaks out of the egg in which it has been growing.

Herbivore

A herbivore is an animal that eats only plants. The opposite of herbivore is carnivore.

Insect

An insect is a small animal with six legs. Ants and bees are insects.

Joint

A joint is the place where two parts of the body join together. You can bend your joints to move your arms, legs and other body parts.

Larva

The larva is the young form of an insect at the stage when it has just hatched from its egg. Larvae is the plural of larva.

Leaves

Leaves are usually flat and green. They grow from stems and branches of plants. Leaves use sunlight, air and water to make food for plants to grow.

Life cycle

A life cycle is the different stages of growth that a living thing passes through in the course of its life. For example, a frog goes through three stages in its life cycle – frogspawn, tadpole and frog.

Living

Living means that something is alive. Living things grow, reproduce and need water and food. Living is the opposite of non-living.

Magnifying glass

A magnifying glass is a piece of curved glass or plastic that makes things look larger when you look through it.

Mammal

A mammal is a warm-bodied animal that feeds its young with milk. Cats, horses, dogs and people are mammals.

Medicine

This is what is given to you when you are ill to make you well again. Medicine can be a tablet or liquid. Only take medicine that has been given to you by a nurse, a doctor, your parents or your carer.

Minerals

Minerals are special substances in the soil that plants need to grow healthy and strong. Minerals are also found in foods, such as salad and fruit juice. Minerals help your body to stay healthy.

Minibeast

A minibeast is a small animal without bones. Bees and worms are minibeasts.

Nature

This is the world around us that includes living things, such as plants and animals.

Nectar

This is a sweet liquid inside flowers that insects and birds like to feed on.

Nocturnal

Nocturnal means happening at night. A nocturnal animal comes out only at night.

Non-living

Non-living means that something is not alive. Things that are not alive do not feed, grow or reproduce, for example, a stone. Non-living is the opposite of living.

Omnivore

An omnivore is an animal that eats both meat and plants.

Pet

A pet is a tame animal that lives in your home. Dogs, cats and guinea pigs are often kept as pets.

Petal

A petal is the large, usually flat part of a flower that attracts insects and birds. Petals are often brightly coloured, with eye-catching markings.

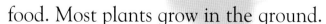

Plant

A plant is a living thing that cannot move around and that makes its own food. Most plants grow in the ground.

Pollen

Pollen is a sticky, yellow powder made by flowers. It has to be carried from one flower to another for seeds to grow. When insects and birds visit flowers to drink nectar, they often pick up pollen.

Protein

This is a special substance found in foods, such as fish and cheese. Protein helps to make your body strong and healthy.

Recycling

Recycling is using things again instead of throwing them away. For example, you can recycle most types of paper, bottles, cans, clothes and plastic.

Reproduce

This is when living things have young. Some animals reproduce by giving birth to live young. Others reproduce by laying eggs. Many plants reproduce by making seeds, which grow into new plants.

Reptile

A reptile is an animal with a cold body and scaly skin. Most reptiles lay eggs. Lizards and snakes are reptiles.

Roots

The roots of a plant grow down into the soil so they can suck up water and minerals. Roots are the first parts of a new plant to grow. They hold the plant firmly in the ground.

Seed

Plants make seeds that will grow into new plants. Each seed contains a tiny plant and enough food for it to start growing. Seeds are carried away from plants by wind, water or animals.

Seedling

This is a baby plant that has grown from a seed.

Sense

Senses are how animals and people find out about the world. People have five senses. We see with our eyes, hear with our ears, smell with our noses, touch with our skin and taste with our tongues.

Shoot

A shoot is the growing part of a stem, bud or leaf. Shoots grow towards the light.

Soil

The mixture of rotted plants, animals and different sized stones in which new plants grow.

Spawn

This is a large group of eggs, usually laid by frogs or fish.

Specimen

A specimen is an object that a scientist studies. The objects in a nature collection are specimens.

Starch

This is a special substance found in foods, such as bread and pasta. Starch helps to give you energy.

Stem

This is the strong, tube-like part of a plant that grows towards the light. The stem supports the plant parts and carries water and minerals to them.

Tadpole

A tadpole is the stage in a frog's life cycle after it has hatched from an egg and before it grows into an adult frog.

Teeth

These are in your mouth and help you to bite and chew food. Teeth are hard and strong. Children have 20 milk teeth, which are replaced by up to 32 teeth as they become adults.

Tree

A plant that has a woody trunk, branches, leaves and roots. Oak, Fir and Eucalyptus are all types of trees. Trees provide homes for many birds and insects.

Vitamins

These are special substances found in foods such as fruit and vegetables. Vitamins help your body to grow and to stay healthy.

Young

This describes the off-spring of living things before they have grown into adults. For example, children are young human beings, lambs are young sheep and puppies are young dogs.

Index

Bye-bye!